Arizona's Haunted Hotspots

Arizona's Haunted Hotspots

Heather Woodward

Schiffer Publishing Ltd

4880 Lower Valley Road, Atglen, Pennsylvania 19310

Photography by Rachel Woodward

Foreword by Richard Senate

Dedication

To Tyler Andrew Ross

The little guy that makes my world go 'round.

Schiffer Books are available at special discounts for bulk purchases for sales promotions or premiums. Special editions, including personalized covers, corporate imprints, and excerpts can be created in large quantities for special needs. For more information contact the publisher:

Published by Schiffer Publishing Ltd.
4880 Lower Valley Road
Atglen, PA 19310
Phone: (610) 593-1777; Fax: (610) 593-2002
E-mail: Info@schifferbooks.com

For the largest selection of fine reference books on this and related subjects,
please visit our website at:
www.schifferbooks.com
We are always looking for people to write books on new and related subjects.
If you have an idea for a book please contact us at the above address.

This book may be purchased from the publisher.
Include $5.00 for shipping.
Please try your bookstore first.
You may write for a free catalog.

In Europe, Schiffer books are distributed by
Bushwood Books
6 Marksbury Ave.
Kew Gardens
Surrey TW9 4JF England
Phone: 44 (0) 20 8392 8585; Fax: 44 (0) 20 8392 9876
E-mail: info@bushwoodbooks.co.uk
Website: www.bushwoodbooks.co.uk

Other Schiffer Books by the Author:
Ghosts of Central Arizona, 978-0-7643-3387-3, $14.99

Other Schiffer Books on Related Subjects:
Scare-Izona: A Travel Guide to Arizona's Spookiest Spots, 978-0-7643-2844-2, $14.95
Southern Arizona's Most Haunted, 978-0-7643-3416-0, $14.99
Tombstone: Relive the Gunfight at the OK Corral, 978-0-7643-3425-2, $9.99

Copyright © 2011 by Heather Woodward
Library of Congress Control Number: 2011927105

Designed by Mark David Bowyer
Type set in A Charming Font Expanded / NewBaskerville BT

ISBN: 978-0-7643-3748-2
Printed in the United States of America

Contents

Acknowledgments

† Dinah, Jennifer, Stacey, and all of the supportive, hard-working folks at Schiffer — thank you for your guidance and making book-writing a positive experience from start to finish

† Richard Senate — thank you for paving the way for future paranormal investigators

† Guy Jackson — thank you for being the adventurous soul you are

† Dad, Lisa, and Mom — thank you for your unyielding support

Foreword

Arizona is a haunted state. Perhaps it's the loneliness of the vast deserts or perhaps it's the people who have called this special land home. Ghosts are extensions of living people, their drive, loyalty, and passions are translated into the many reports and activities of Arizona's persistent ghosts. There is also a link to death. Places where people have suffered often harbor phantoms. It is as if the soul was trying to reconcile itself to its new unknown state in the afterlife. I have visited the state of Arizona and I will confirm that the author is correct in saying it is a ghost-ridden place where the past and present seem to co-mingle from time to time.

I began my quest to understand specters and haunted places on a warm July night in 1978. I was part of an archaeological team out of Cal Poly San Luis Obispo digging at the old Spanish Mission San Antonio de Padua in California. That night, while walking in the courtyard, something remarkable happened to me. I saw what appeared to be a monk. It was dressed in brown robe and cowl, walking across the courtyard with a candle. When I approached him, believing it was a member of the Franciscan Order still attached to the Mission, it simply vanished before my eyes.

I wasn't looking for it, and I didn't really know what I had witnessed, but I saw something I couldn't rationally explain. It slowly dawned on me that it was one of those ghosts that they talk about. Only then did I become frightened. I asked around and others had seen phantoms there as well. From that day on, I have been a ghost hunter, investigating sites all over the southwest, Hawaii and England. It was a different world back in the late 1970s and early 1980s. Today ghost hunting is popular and accepted but when I started out, it was not. I faced many prejudices and more than a few friends and family thought I was off my rocker. There were few books on the subject around then. Hans Holzer's books and those of Suzie Smith were about the only ones in print. There were no acceptable ways to investigate a haunted site or even tools to use.

Psychic research hadn't progressed much beyond the 1920s. Still, slowly, I developed ways to operate and I networked with some really great people. They showed me the how to do this as a science and not a hobby; such greats as Dr. Thelma Moss (a giant in the field) and D. Scott Rogo helped me to understand that ghosts are really a complex subject. On the metaphysical side, I owe a great debt to Dr. Edward Foard of Santa Barbara, a Spiritualist Minster of the Lillydale School, who showed me that science couldn't answer all of the questions. He was a great man and a credit to his religion. He has passed on now, or as he might say, journeyed to Summerland. Another who helped me in those years was Dr. Kenny Kingston, a psychic with a great heart.

I didn't really have a plan when I started out, just a vague goal to discover all I could about ghosts and their ways. I wanted to know what they were and why they were here.

I still cannot answer the question: what are ghosts? Safe to say, they are phenomena as yet unexplained, but one universal to all mankind. Every time I develop or embrace a theory about ghosts, it seems to turn to dust as more data comes forth.

What do I know? Not all ghosts seem to be spirits of the dead, but a small minority might be. Some ghosts might be holes in the fabric of time, but not all, some may well be projections of the mind, created by living people, but not in every case. Some may even be evil, demonic creatures, but these seem few and far between. Trying to find firm data is like walking on Jell-O — there are lots of theories and few facts. One thing is clear; too many people have seen too many things over the centuries to discount them. There is something out there and it commands us to investigate further.

Ghosts present us with many questions and few answers but they might give us clues to the greatest question of them all: do we survive death itself? If ghosts do exist, then there is no death!

When I began this unique quest, I was fully committed to finding a scientific rational for ghosts, some new element that would explain ghostly behavior. This answer has eluded me. As the years progressed I have been pulled more and more into a belief that the psychics and metaphysicians might have the answer after all. Ghosts are much more than an anomaly and more spiritual than a blip on an "e-meter."

In 1989, I investigated the Oatman Hotel in Arizona. I always say I spent a week in Oatman in a single day. There is definitely something at the old hotel, now a museum. Is it the ghost of Clark Gable and Carol Lombard? I think not. They were the most famous persons to spend a night at the old adobe structure, but I feel the ghost is that of a former staff member. I have felt the distinct chill on the second floor of the place and heard the walking sounds on the floorboards when there was no one there. It is worthy of investigation and a place I wouldn't mind going back to in the future.

The Jerome Hotel, formerly a hospital, stands as an ideal place to look for ghosts. Many seek out the mysterious Lady in White who walks the halls. The ghost town of Jerome is a place where the spirits of the dead seem to outnumber the living. The whole of the mining town is seeped with history and I feel it may well be a vortex where the past and present seem to come together. If you are looking for ghosts, spend a week here and your chances of an encounter are good. The old brothel, called the House of Joy, is where I saw something supernatural look out the window when I visited the town. Many places of prostitution are haunted all over the world from Pompeii to Carson City, Nevada. It might have something to do with the passions of the occupation or the violence and loneliness of the "working girls" who labored in these establishments. Many did take their own lives; these acts of self-destruction are more than enough to cause ghosts to walk. Yes, Jerome is truly haunted.

The old Mission of San Francisco del Bac near Tucson is a magnificent structure, called "the white dove of the desert." It is, like many of the Old Spanish Missions, haunted by ghostly padres, still doing their work as missionaries. I collected a great many stories of the ghosts seen at this place and even toured the grounds late at night. The small mortuary chapel seems to be the center of activity as is the bell tower, where a ghost padre still labors to finish the tower.

Many places in Arizona are haunted, from the old adobes to modern buildings. All are discussed in Heather's book, with all the data needed by ghost seekers or folklorists. This work is a must-have volume for anyone who is interested in the supernatural. I recommend it without reservation. Read the stories, visit the sites and be ready for that drop in temperature linked to haunted places. Keep an eye out for that flash of light or movement out of the corner of your eye... it could well be a ghost. Be wary of a sudden smell that shouldn't be there for smells can be manifest by spirits, and listen well for the footsteps on hardwood floors or the mumbled voices of the long dead.

Happy ghost hunting!

—Richard Senate, Ventura, California
Author, *Ghosts of the Haunted Coast*
www.ghost-stalker.com

Introduction

Ghost Folklore

When I explain that I am a professional psychic and profiler for a living, people are often at first shocked and then eventually become keenly curious. Regularly, on radio shows I am asked how I decided that a career in the supernatural is even a possibility or how I even came to consider it?

For me, I don't think I ever had a choice. There were points in my life where I thought I did and decided to take the road akin to corporate life — or at least my small town version of it. Yes, at one point I wore blazers and sat in an office all day. In fact, for most of my adult working career I was a clock-watcher. I enjoyed the aspect of going to work every day, but I couldn't stand the mundane eight-hour routine. Nor could I stand office politics. On my days off, I was grumpy and life became a chore, but I stuck with it for years because I felt like I had to prove to myself, and everyone else, that I was traditionally successful.

Sometimes, I go back across the timeline in my life and look for that one moment where I lost my footing and decided that I was going to try and please everyone, but I don't think there is a pivotal moment. I think it's a progression of small compromises that eventually turned into a bigger lifestyle change I wasn't even aware I was making. It didn't come up on me like a slap in face. It was more of a slow, deliberate descent into complacency.

My psychic abilities kicked in when I was about five years old. I remember "seeing" people, places, and events that weren't necessarily there and that didn't bother me. I had no concept of lateral thinking and it didn't faze me that not everything had a static temporal continuation. My visitations were always heavily immersed with Biblical symbolism. I attended a private Christian school and went to Sunday Bible study every weekend. My parents sent me to Christian summer camps, sometimes even weekend winter camps. I was heavily immersed in the fire and brimstone of the Baptist faith. It was a weird world of suffering, strength and sin. My belief in God was powerful and I knew that he existed and he would take care of me in some capacity.

Sometimes, I wish I could get back that strength of belief that I had at that age. There was no questioning faith or God or what he had come to do for me. I understood his need to die on the cross and be resurrected. There was no doubt in my mind that every story my Bible schoolteachers told me were true accounts. In fact, I was having my own visions of the time that fueled my belief further.

I have a strong recollection of one of my very first visitations. The memory is as sharp and vivid as if it happened yesterday. I was playing by myself. It was nighttime and I'm not even sure why I was up. Perhaps, that's partly why my siblings weren't around. They were still little and probably asleep. In the darkness I remember seeing a bright white light. The light shifted and turned into a silhouette. The image in front of me looked human but it was massive and it had wings.

I gaped at the large white creature in front of me with awe. It didn't seem to want to harm me but there was something grotesque about its form. Looking closer I realized its wings were covered in eyes that blinked at random intervals. The eyeballs really freaked me out and I didn't like that they were staring at me.

In my five-year-old head, I came upon the realization that I was having a visitation from an angel. Strangely, this put me at ease because if it was an angel then it was of God and therefore I knew I wasn't going to Hell. I felt honored that an angel would take time out from its busy schedule to hang out with me. On the other hand, I wasn't quite sure what it wanted and I was little bit afraid that it had something to do with its peering eyeballs.

From there my memory fades away into blackness. I'm not sure if I talked to it or if it had a message for me. I'm sure if it did I blocked it out of my mind. Not because I don't believe that it happened but because of the sure magnitude of the memory itself. If I were to think about what the implications of an angel coming to a child at such a young age... Well, it's the stuff of Biblical proportions. To this day I'm not sure if I was chosen or damned. There are huge points in my life where I could argue both sides.

However, the religious visitations didn't stop there. I was in the back of my parent's car. My father was driving and we were heading toward the 101 freeway. We were veering left merging into an intersection. The mall was to my back, the Arby's to my right. Something told me to look up and, without reservation, I did... In the sky, billowy clouds puffed up like marshmallows and two shining towers of gold peeked through from the softness. As I got a better look, I realized that the two gold posts were holding up long bars of gold. In the middle there was a latch.

In an instant, I knew that I was staring at the gates of Heaven and it perplexed me. I remember looking away for a moment and then staring up again. The gold towers were gone and I was sad to see them go. I remember turning around and staring out the back window hoping to get another glimpse of Heaven, but I never did.

Now, I'm not sure which experience seems more far-fetched. For me, because of other experiences in my life, I am more apt to believe I was visited by an angel than the idea that I saw Heaven. I guess it's easier for me to comprehend an entity than a place where good people go if they let God into their hearts and try not to sin. Besides, I have a sneaky suspicion the alleged angel was the first contact with my spirit guide.

I can't tell you what the glimpse of Heaven means, except that maybe at one time I was symbiotic with my purpose. Perhaps, like a very strange version of "LOST", I was having visitations by strange beings and having visions that were supposed to send me on a focused journey. Somewhere, however, I crashed on an island and I am still trying to find my way back to the importance of that vision — to connect with that sense of true purpose. I think that's what we all strive for in some small way. We wouldn't be here if we didn't have some investment into the outcome.

I grew up with ghosts too. My family lived in more haunted houses than ones that weren't. I often wonder if it's my family who is haunted. Maybe it's not so much the structures, but the energies of those that dwell within. My parents took in stride, though and never questioned the nature of the disembodied footsteps, the opening and closing of doors, the knocks and weird physical manifestations. In one house a ghost produced some sort of viscous substance that I can only equate to ectoplasm. It was thick and slimy and substantial. It left wet spots on the floor and on the walls.

You would think with that sort of activity someone in the house would be freaked out, but my family was used to that sort of thing. It was a common, a natural occurrence that seemed to come and go as it pleased. I don't know why we didn't have enough sense to be afraid. Instead there was an overall acceptance, resilience to the paranormal. It lived with us like a pet or an eccentric uncle.

Because it was commonplace, it's not a far leap to suggest that in my teens I would be highly curious of the origins of the activity in the places I lived. By this time, my parents had divorced but that still didn't change the paranormal phenomenon. Now, there were twice as many incidents, two households to fill with supernatural antics.

It was about this time I found the wonderful world of witchcraft and all it had to offer. Adding that to my already healthy curiosity about spirits and it's vaguely obvious as to what happened next. I became obsessed with talking boards and the idea of spirit communication. I bought an

Ouija board. It didn't have the full effect I wanted, so I made my own from a bathroom mirror, etching the letters with a chemical composite that left a frosted imprint in the glass. My friends and I started our own home circle and used our mirror as a talking board and a shot glass as a planchette. Sometimes, we used a highball glass. It didn't matter. The minute we got near the board, the glass planchette vibrated. All I had to do was lightly touch it for it to slide wildly across the board. It worked a little too well, so I stopped using it and left it at a friend's house.

I kept the Parker Brothers Ouija board in my bedroom hidden in my closet. It didn't work as well and it seemed safer. My mother hated the thing and vowed that if she ever found it she would burn it. I was never very good at putting away my clothes, so I hid it under my dirty laundry. At night, I would hear it jiggling in my closet, beckoning me to play with it. Sometimes, I would waken to the box knocking against the walls of my bedroom. It was loud and obnoxious, but nobody in our house seemed to hear it but me. For a time, I thought I was going crazy. However, it all ended rather quickly because my mom found it and took outside to burn it — or rather she tried to burn it. It took her a couple of tries. Mostly it just smoldered and then went out. This both scared and frustrated her, so she kept at it until she finally got it to catch fire. It was the weirdest site when it burned. I've never seen anything burn green. Yes, green.

To this day I'm not sure why my mother was freaked out about the green burning Ouija board and paid no attention to the weird dark figure that prowled around in our house. If my sister got home from school before us she would sit outside on the front steps until somebody else was home. The dark shadow didn't bother my mother, but the spirit communication did. Later, I found out that I lived less than a mile from the underground caves where the Manson family used to hang out. Further up the road a woman was tortured, raped, stripped of her clothes and chained to a crumbling wall. The police found her dead body days later. I have no idea who the dark figure was but I can tell you that it sprang from evil. That whole neighborhood was cursed.

Years went by and I got more and more into divination. I started playing around with tarot cards and giving readings. It was fun for me, though I never took it too seriously. I treated it like a parlor game. In my twenties, I met someone who would change my views forever. He was a love interest. Someone who came into my life rather quickly and then just as quickly faded away. He was ten years older than me and dangerously sexy. The man was in a punk band, had recorded a few records, and was bad to the bone. I was instantly in love with him. We had this otherworldly connection that I had never felt with anyone else. It was the first time I had ever felt a true soul connection.

It just so happens he was into magick and was a damn good tarot reader. He told me that I needed to practice my tarot skills more and use them. So, in the name of giddy capricious love, I bought as many books as I could find on the subject and started studying tarot. I was veracious with the practice and incorporated the tarot cards in my spell work. Like all ill-fated relationships ours went south very quickly. It descended like any good punk rock relationship should. There was enough hedonistic drama fit for a movie and it turned ugly really fast.

However, I held a torch for him for way too many years. Mostly because I had found something in him that I hadn't in anyone else — passion. We had the same raw, unbridled passion for magick and the supernatural. Until then I had never met anyone who was so wholly immersed in it and so unabashedly willing to talk about it.

A couple of years later I had my son and started to focus more on giving readings professionally. Still, I never had the nerve to stand proud and own it, but I gave readings to family and friends. I took classes and read all I could about divination techniques. More than that my psychic abilities started to kick in heavily to the point where it was almost unbearable. My focus on tarot had opened my sixth sense and I was gathering information from universal consciousness at an alarming rate. Due to this I questioned anyone and everyone I could on psychic development. I read books and started to devise a system that would slow down the process for me and give me some control over my abilities. It was like shooting in the dark. I had no idea what I was doing but eventually it all came together and I realized that I destined to be a psychic.

Of course, I fought it for years. I did my best to ignore that side of myself and live a "normal" life, which didn't work. Eventually, I gave in and started a paranormal investigation group. Paranormal drama ensued and I forgot how fun it was to investigate, so I gave up the group mentality and started investigating with some of my friends who were in the field. The ghost hunting turned into an obsession and I dedicated my weekends to finding haunted locations to investigate.

This didn't sit well with my husband and my son who resented the time away from them. I worked all week and the weekends were supposed to be dedicated to the family. However, for me, the weekends were the only time I felt like I was doing something for myself. I didn't realize at the time, but during those investigations I felt integrated. I felt happy. I thought it was because I liked ghost hunting. Upon reflection I realize that it was the only time I was truly myself. I felt safe to be a psychic and it felt right.

I think it is appropriate to tell you that my marriage failed for various reasons. Don't worry ghost hunting isn't cited as the reason I got divorced. It was just a symptom of a larger problem. I was so miserable and I couldn't figure out why my life had taken such a horrible turn. One day I literally packed up all of my things and moved to Tucson, Arizona. Within three weeks of being here, I was offered a contract from Schiffer Publishing to write my first book about ghosts. Yes, my first book would be about ghosts.

It was a cathartic moment for me. It was the first time I really felt like I accepted all parts of myself. With that knowledge there has been some harsh lessons. The past two years have probably been the hardest years in my life. Ever. The transformation has been daunting and extremely painful but honest and liberating at the same time.

Each one of my books has been an adventure. Not just because of the haunted locations, but because each investigation has been a moment in my life where I have accepted and embraced my role as a psychic. Being honest enough write it down in a book and share it with the world for better or for worse — that's why I write about my own experiences. It's also why I can't just write the ghost stories and leave it at that. These books are about the journey of the human experience…my journey and, hopefully, it will be yours as well.

The Folklore Aspect

Ghosts are as old as man. Every human culture has an interpretation woven into their mythology. From the Scottish "wraith" to the Germanic "poltergeist" to the Shamanistic "fetch" they all seem to have one thing in common. They are souls of unrest and generally only come in two classifications: good and evil.

Throughout history, in most parts of the world, the presence of a ghost was considered an ominous omen or a sign of unfinished business. Systematic death rituals were put into place to remedy the superstition.

Ancient burial rituals and the veneration of the dead, particularly ancestral worship, were implemented as part of the cultural belief system. The practice was based on the belief that deceased family members went on in the afterlife to aid their living relatives. Depending on the care of the dead, the existing family would either reap a positive life or suffer the consequences. To keep favor with deceased ancestors also meant that you could ask for assistance from the spirit world in times of need or hardship. To honor your ancestors in death meant you were honored in life. It was looked upon as a call of duty and also insurance for existing relatives and their predecessors.

There was another reason to keep the dead happy and content during the afterlife: so that an ancestor did not become starved or jealous of the living, thereby becoming an evil or maligned spirit. Due to this many burial rituals incorporated some sort of custom of sacrifice or feeding of their ancestors to keep them nourished and happy. Honor and respect were also given through prayer and repetitive visits to the burial grounds.

As time went on, the traditional meaning of a ghost evolved through folklore. It was believed that ghosts were imprisoned souls bound to earth by the bad deeds they had done or vengeful persons who were looking for vindication and chose to stay on the earthly plane. In many cultures the appearance of a ghost portended a death.

According too many beliefs, the soul was an exact replica of the person in an air-like form stored in the body. Many assumed that a person's breath was a part of that soul. In colder seasons and climates the breath could be seen as a milky white substance coming from the body. When a spirit left the body it took on the form of a cold breath. There were many superstitions around going outside on a cold night for fear that your soul would leave your body accidentally through your breath.

Ghosts were thought to be composed of an airy or wispy material, dressed in the clothing they died in. Throughout most traditional accounts in folklore white ladies were commonly spotted in rural areas. They were women who had died tragically; usually at the hand of their husbands who had murdered or betrayed them. A white lady was considered a harbinger of death. Someone in the immediate family lineage was to die.

In modern times, the white lady myth still lives on. She is immortalized in many ghost tales and urban legends. No matter what the geographical location the Lady in White ghost story has its similarities. She is a distraught young woman in a white wedding or prom dress wandering on the edge of a dark and rural road in the middle of the night. A man driving by spots her and offers her a ride worried for her safety. Usually, the man later recalls that the reason he noticed the Lady in White was because she didn't seem to fit the scenery. There was something odd about her that didn't seem right. Later, the man realizes that when first seeing the woman she didn't have any defining features or skin tone. Only in the car did she seem to have life-like characteristics.

In the car, the conversation is strangled or eerily quiet. The only words spoken are directions to their destination. When the Lady in White gets out of the car she walks a few feet and then disappears. Confused, the man walks to the front door of the house or building looking for answers from anyone who happens to be there. Only then does he find out the truth: the woman is really the ghost of a woman who has been killed horribly in a car accident or by her significant other.

There are other manifestations of the Lady in White. She doesn't wander in rural areas. Instead, she floats down the corridors of historical hotels. The descriptions are always the same. She is a younger woman in her mid-twenties to mid-thirties dawned in period clothing. Some describe her as French but always she is genteel, refined and sweet.

Again, most of the sightings are from men. They are intrigued by her sullen or grieving countenance as she walks near them without saying a word. A compulsion sets in but before the man can ask the lady and white what she needs she disappears. Floral or lavender perfume lingering behind is the only remembrance of her existence.

In British folklore, spirits were said to be formed by excessive grieving by the living. Holding on to the person's memory forced the dead person's soul to become trapped to the earthly plane and inhibited a peaceful rest. Another superstition claimed a person would be haunted by their dead lover if they took another before performing some sort of ritual of release. Perhaps these superstitions have some validity to them. Perhaps these Lady in White apparitions are the manifestations of excessive grief or the lack of a release ritual. Perhaps the living gives life energy to the personality consciousness of the dead.

By the 1800s, ghosts were well implemented in the folklore of every culture throughout the world. The idea of communication with spirits was frowned upon because of the implications of a ghost having a mostly bad connotation, but during the nineteenth century things would change in the Western cultures. A spiritual renaissance emerged. Necromancy and other occult practices became more widely accepted in the metropolitan areas of Europe and the United States. Communicating with the deceased would become a household topic from the discovery of two sisters…

The Fox Sisters – (L to R) Margaret, Catherine, and Leah circa 1852.
Library of Congress ID#cph 3a06258. *Public Domain*.

Part I

The History of Spiritualism

The Fox Sisters

In 1848, the act of spirit communication took a turn for the better with the rise of Spiritualism. Connecting with the deceased no longer had the negative connotation of an omen or portent of death. Instead, it became a modern day practice founded on the concept that a ghost was the non-corporeal aspect of a person after death. It hinged on the belief that there was life after death and that the dearly departed wanted to communicate with their living counterparts. Spirit communication became an act of love rather than a something to be feared.

The Spiritualism Movement was started in a cottage in Hydesville, New York, by Maggie and Kate Fox, the two youngest daughters of John Fox, whose extraverted communication with a resident ghost became that of legend. However, there were circling rumors that the home was haunted years before the Fox family moved in. A point that later skeptics would use as evidence that the Fox sisters were frauds.

The story of the cottage's haunted history began with the Bell couple that resided there from 1843-1844. Toward the last few months of their stay in the cottage, Mrs. Bell's hired a young local woman name Lucretia Pulver to be her maid. Ms. Pulver cooked, cleaned, and managed most of the household duties.

One day, Charles B Rosma, a peddler selling pots, pans, and other kitchen utensils, paid a visit to the Bell residence. Mrs. Bell bought a few items and although, it was not customary for the time, the couple invited the peddler to stay at their home for a number of days.

Sometime between the time the peddler stayed at the home and when he left, Ms. Pulver was relieved of her duties as a maid. No specific reasons were given for the girl's dismissal, but it seemed to be amicable. There were no arguments or disputes and Mrs. Bell even went so far as to drive the woman home in their wagon. Before she was dismissed, Ms. Pulver purchased a knife from the peddler with instruction to deliver the piece of cutlery to her father's farm. The knife never made it to its destination and Mr. Rosma was never seen again.

A week later, Mrs. Bell asked Ms. Pulver to resume her position performing household duties. Bewildered but grateful, the girl gladly took her job back and again moved her belongings into the Bell's cottage. On her first day back working in the home the maid noticed something odd: Charles B. Rosma was nowhere to be found, but the peddler's merchandise was still there. Giving the benefit of the doubt, the girl assumed that Mrs. Bell had purchased the rest of the peddler's items and thought nothing of it.

The maid fell into her old routine easily. However, something in the house had changed and it seemed that Ms. Pulver became the target. Frequently, she heard knocking noises and tapping sounds coming from the empty room where the peddler had stayed during his visit. The sound of footsteps kept her up at nights. The maid claimed she could hear them traipsing through the house and then descending down the stairs into the cellar.

The events became more superstitious when one afternoon Ms. Pulver had to go into the cellar. As she descended to the bottom of the stairs, she tripped over a mound of newly turned earth. Mrs. Bell heard the commotion and came down to check on the girl. Slightly jarred, the maid seemed fine. She was more befuddled by the mound of dirt than the shock of the fall. Mrs. Bell explained away the mound by declaring there were "rat holes" that needed to be covered up. The maid accepted the practical explanation for the pile of earth and resumed her duties.

Weeks went by and the paranormal activity in the house didn't stop. The knocks and unexplained noises seemed to come with more frequency and fervor. Frightened and unnerved, Ms. Pulver routinely asked her brother to stay with her while she did her chores. Usually, in his company the activity would dissipate, but on certain occasions the noises in the house would grow louder and more frequent. This happened one too many times and the girl's brother left in a panic refusing to step foot in the house ever again. Shortly after, the Bell couple moved out of the cottage and the root of the paranormal activity was never explained.

In 1844, the Weekman family and their relative, Mrs. Lafe, moved into the Hydesville cottage. However, their stay was very short due to the loud knocking and unexplained noises that plagued the home.

One afternoon, Mrs. Lafe walked into the kitchen and screamed in terror at the sight before her. When the Weekman family came to her to find out what all the commotion was about, she claimed to have spotted the apparition of a tall man in a frock coat standing in the middle of the kitchen. He vanished just as quickly as he had appeared.

Shortly after the incident in the kitchen, all members of the household heard the wandering footsteps and the mysterious knockings. Sometimes the paranormal phenomenon manifested during the day, but it seemed relentlessness at night. The Weekmans frequently complained of not sleeping and soon the constant noises became too troublesome; the family promptly moved out of the cottage.

In 1848, when John Fox moved his family into the house, it is unclear if he knew about the prior stories of paranormal activity. Taking residence at the cottage was supposed to be temporary while their new home was being built on a newly purchased property nearby, so whether or not he had heard the stories was a moot point since he didn't plan on staying at the property for too long. Besides, being a pragmatic man, he would have passed the ghost tales off as the workings of an over-active imagination.

John Fox and his wife Margaret had two daughters still living with them: Margaret (Maggie) Fox was nine years old while her sister, Katherine (Kate), was eleven years old. The girls were thought to be free-spirited and outspoken for the time period. This was, in part, due to the fact they were the last of six children raised by the couple who were in the prime years of their life by the time the two girls were born. Kate and Maggie were far younger than their other siblings. Leah, their eldest sister, was more than twenty years their senior and she had her own daughter who was near the same age as the two girls.

Maggie and Kate were the product of their parent's reconciliation. In the earlier years, John was an alcoholic and a gambler. Willful Margaret chose to leave her husband and suffer poverty and the social stigma rather than deal with his drinking. She raised her four other children in near poverty making ends meet wherever she could. Still, she figured the hardship was better than living with an abusive drunk.

Years later, John sobered up and Margaret took him back. They eventually remarried and had two more children together, Kate and Maggie. John farmed to support his family and made a decent living. The Fox's were by no means wealthy or middle class, but John strived to make amends and keep food on the table.

Almost as soon as the Fox family moved into the Hydesville cottage, the knockings and unexplained noises took over. Banging sounds and rattling noises kept everyone up at night. Margaret and the two girls complained to John that the disembodied sounds were frightening. Being a methodical, practical man, John rationalized the noises as the regular sounds of the house settling spurred on by female hysteria and childish, wild imaginations. He took little stock in the claims and ignored their concerns.

However, soon the paranormal activity would escalate from passive noise to physical force. One night, a hysterical Kate woke up screaming in terror claiming a cold hand had stroked her face. In the same room, a frightened Maggie swore that the blankets were ripped off her bed by invisible hands. Their mother chimed in by explaining that she had been hearing disembodied footsteps stomp through the house and then descend into the cellar. She could not sleep because she was anxious about who or what could be creeping through the house.

Concerned but still unfazed by their claims, John went around the house searching for a logical, plausible explanation for the phenomenon. Nightly, he would check the house for anything weird or unexplained, but he never found anything that could debunk the paranormal activity. His empty pursuits fueled his daughters' belief that there was a true apparition in the house. The more John claimed the footsteps and noises were practical in nature the more his wife and two girls believed they were being haunted. Superstition kicked in and the girls even went so far as to call the ghost, "Mr. Splitfoot," a nickname for the Devil.

On March 31, 1848, the knocks in the house kept on through the night and into the next day. John was convinced he would be able to find the source of the noises and each time he heard a knock he would search the house. When he thought he came near an area where the disembodied sound manifested itself, he knocked back hoping to mimic what he was hearing. As time went on Kate realized that the house would respond with the same amount of knocks that her father knocked in his tireless and fruitless search for the unexplained noises. It was almost as if "Mr. Splitfoot" was trying to communicate with John to let him know that, indeed, he was a spirit.

Kate explained her observations to her sister and her mother and they decided to test the theory. Margaret and her two girls listened for John's knocking, hoping that "Mr. Splitfoot" would reply with the same amount of knockings. Within seconds a reply in the form of knocks reverberated through the house. Excited and inspired, Kate decided to take matters into her own hands and try her theory on her own terms. With her sister and mother watching, Kate wrangled up the nerve to speak to the ghost directly.

"Here, Mr. Splitfoot, do as I do!" Kate asserted.

The girl clapped her hands together two times. Within seconds she was answered with the same amount of knocks somewhere in the house from an indistinct location. Everyone in the room was in awe of how quickly and easily the ghost had communicated with the girl. Repeating the process, Kate knocked on the wall and instantly Mr. Splitfoot mimicked her.

Eventually John joined his wife in Kate and Maggie's small room. He was amazed and with the rest of the family watched Kate communicate with "Mr. Splitfoot" through claps and knocks. Now that there was a baseline for the activity, Margaret decided that she would test the apparition to see if it was a true spirit. She believed that if it were real then "he" would know information that only she or other family members would know. Margaret asked the ghost to tap out the ages of her other grown children who were not present. One by one, the entity rapped the ages of the other members of the Fox family with chilling accuracy. The family was convinced they were indeed communicating with an authentic spirit. How could the ghost know the ages of people he had never met?

Dumbfounded, John went to his neighbor's house, the Redfields, to ask them to experience the phenomenon of the disembodied knocking. The Redfields walked over to the house fully skeptical of John's claims that Kate was communicating with a spirit. They crammed into the girls' room and asked a series of questions that no one knew the answers to. Each time "Mr. Splitfoot" answered their inquiries with the precise amount of knocks. After that experience the neighbors were instant believers.

The news about the supernatural happenings at the Hydesville cottage traveled with lightning speed. Soon, neighbors and other travelers were visiting the house at all hours of the day and night to experience the phenomenon and to communicate with the spirit. One visitor, William Duesler, a past resident of the cottage, had the idea to communicate with the entity using a more structured format so that more complex questions could be asked. He was able to design a system using a certain number of knocks that corresponded with a specific letter of the alphabet. Also, the answers "yes" and "no" were designated by a series of raps. This way with the growing pool of people asking questions the answers could be decoded more simply and accurately.

Curious as to the true identity of "Mr. Splitfoot," Duesler began asking the ghost personal questions about his presence at the Hydesville cottage. Spectators were astonished when the entity declared himself to be Charles B. Rosma — the peddler who had gone missing just years before.

Coincidentally, Lucretia Pulver, the young woman who had worked as a maid for the Bell family, was in the room at the time of the declaration. Astonished, she conveyed the story about her tripping on the mound of dirt in the cellar. This time the tale held a more sinister tone. She surmised that perhaps she had fallen on the very spot that the poor peddler had been buried after he had been cruelly murdered.

Compelled by the new knowledge, in the summer months after the March incident, John Fox and William Duesler took shovels to the cellar and dug in the spot that Lucretia had described. After an hour of backbreaking work, the men were discouraged. They questioned whether the story of the peddler was true or the tall-tale of a mischievous ghost.

Determined to get to the bottom of the paranormal activity once and for all, Fox decided to dig for a little more time. His persistence paid off when the shovel blade hit something hard.

Fox picked up the object the blade hit to give it a better look. It appeared to be a small piece of fragmented bone with strands of hair still affixed to it. With renewed enthusiasm, Fox and Duesler dug deeper into the ground of the cellar. They didn't find anymore human remains, but discovered a few pieces of tattered clothing. Later, the bone fragment was analyzed by a doctor who stated that it was part of a human skull.

With proof that there was a body in the cellar, it was just enough evidence needed for the growing crowds (and the Fox family) to believe that, indeed, the house was haunted by the murdered peddler — that he was, in fact, the entity keeping the family up at night with the noises, the knocks, and the disembodied footsteps that led into the cellar where his body was buried and who now was communicating with the Fox girls creating a movement that would change the way the world looked at spirit communication forever.

The Rise of the Spiritualism Movement

The incident at the Hydesville cottage became that of legend. The many visitors who had witnessed the conversations between the two Fox girls and the ghost, which was now believed to be the murdered peddler, told the amazing story to anyone who would listen.

Kate and Maggie Fox were purported to have mediumistic abilities and could possibly communicate with other willing spirits — and they were quickly sought out for spirit communication sessions in theatres and halls throughout the East Coast and other metropolitan areas. They traveled with their mother and their older sister, Leah, a divorcee earning a living by teaching piano lessons to middle and upper class children to provide for her daughter. Leah soon realized that she, too, could communicate with the spirits using the same rapping techniques as her two younger siblings. She acted as a manager and chaperone for the two girls and often participated in the medium demonstrations. By November 1849, the three sisters were traveling the country performing public displays of spirit communication. In the evening they packed large theaters with spectators full of curiosity and awe. During the day they hosted private sessions for eager paying customers who could afford their lucrative fee.

With the rising fame of the Fox sisters, many others aimed to cash in by declaring they could communicate with spirits too. Some were legitimate mediums that finally had the courage to utilize their natural-born gifts. However, most were charlatans who exploited the venue to make a quick buck. Though the movement gave way to other concepts, such as mysticism, higher consciousness, and the afterlife, it also was a time of cunning and fraud. More than not it was only a matter of time before a medium was denounced by the different committees testing their abilities for any sort of trickery. Still, there was a huge part of the society that undoubtedly believed in the act of communicating with spirit despite the evidence of trickery — and there were those who never gave mediums a fair chance even after certain mediums were able to prove that they were the general article. The pendulum swayed on both extremes and there were very few who were ambivalent about the movement.

Either way, the concept of spirit communication intrigued the masses — whether they were a believer or a skeptic. Demonstrations of spirit communication became a popular form of entertainment especially to the upper middle class and the rich. The key to a successful sitting depended largely on the use of showmanship and tangible evidence. Mediums were wildly competitive with each other and whoever had the best show at the time had the most followers and brought in the most money.

The bulk of mediums were women. This was largely due to the fact that it was a respectful way of making a living in a culture where women had little rights or job opportunities. Medium demonstrations were one of the only forums where women could speak among a mixed audience. While conducting a séance the medium fell under the trance of a spirit that used the human body to communicate in any matter that seemed fitting even if it was shocking or unconventional. Women were considered the more delicate sex, easily swayed, and so it would seem the most logical conclusion that a woman would be more easily used as a conduit for the other side and that they had no awareness of their actions and therefore could not be held responsible for them.

The term "medium" became an umbrella term for anyone who claimed to have the ability to communicate with the deceased. Most mediums were classified under two categories: message mediums and physical mediums. Message mediums fell into a trance state letting the spirit use their voice and body to articulate their messages from the other side while Physical mediums were able to effect their environment by creating paranormal phenomena including ectoplasm.

Presently, most investigators mistake mists and other similar naturally occurring phenomena for ectoplasm when it has no resemblance. In 1894, Charles Richet coined the term ectoplasm to describe the thick, viscous substance that was excreted from a medium's orifice (nose, mouth, ear, belly button, and reproductive parts) and morphed into supernatural extremities, faces, and even a full-bodied apparition. Reports have described it as being warm to the touch, having a doughy or gauze-like texture and smelled of ozone. Ectoplasm oozed from the medium in various forms including a vapor to a stringy membrane to a heavy mass. It was often only seen in the dark and when the lights were turned on it would snap back into the medium and disappear.

During the first séances many mimicked the knocking system used by the Fox Sisters. However, the spirit alphabet quickly became archaic because it was tedious and time consuming without much showmanship. As other mediums joined the forces of spirit communicators, new modalities (and creative hoaxes) were implemented until there was a basic setup for a séance.

A medium would conduct a séance at a private establishment or home. The participants, an equal number of men and women, sat close together around a table. They laid their hands on the table, either clasping their neighbor's hand or splaying their fingers flat so that everyone's fingers touched. Lights were turned down or completely turned off. It was believed that a spirit could be seen more clearly without light. Usually, the discarnate showed itself as a white or luminescent shadowy figure that would glow in the darkness. Other forms of spirit communication included levitating tables, objects moving and disembodied voices.

There were unspoken rules about conducting a séance. A séance could last no longer than two hours unless the spirit requested more time. No more than three séances could be held during a one-week period. The sitters could not touch the conjured spirit or any physical manifestations (like ectoplasm) during a séance unless the spirit first initiated the contact. Without "permission" from the spirit it was feared that the medium or the sitter could be the victim of a severe injury especially when ectoplasm was present. With the extreme snap-back nature of ectoplasm it was thought that the substance could harm the medium if he or she was unnecessarily shocked back into consciousness. Due to this, under no circumstances was the medium to be touched while in a trance state or he or she could risk sickness, insanity or even death.

The Davenport Brothers

As a precaution, some mediums started to use spirit cabinets. A "cabinet" was sometimes an actual piece of furniture but most times it was an area of the room that was curtained off. It was considered a spiritual battery where the medium could attract and manipulate the supernatural forces that were being manifested without worrying about an over-zealous participant.

The spirit cabinet was first used by the Spiritualist duo, the Davenport Brothers, who got the idea from an audience member who asked if they could manifest phenomenon in a sealed container so that there was no form of tampering. The brothers thought the idea was ingenious and the story goes that they contacted their family spirit guide, John King, to aide them in the schematics and measurements for their spirit cabinet. Quickly, the duo added the box to their performances and soon it became an essential part of a séance.

MR IRA DAVENPORT.   MR FAY.   MR COOPER.   MR WM DAVENPORT.

The Davenport Brothers and their Spirit Cabinet.
Public Domain.

Home Circles

As the Spiritualism movement spread, there were many people who wanted to participate in a séance, but didn't have the means or the access to medium performances or a private sitting. Home circles consisted of a group of family and friends who got together at a private home and used simple tools and methods for spirit communication.

Table tipping was the most popular way to contact a spirit. The group would sit around the table with their hands flat on its surface. Concentrating, everyone waited for the table to show signs of movement. Usually, the table vibrated or rocked slowly from side-to-side. As it picked up momentum, the group would ask the spirit to communicate through the table by rocking in a certain pattern for a specific answer. Sometimes the table would knock against the floor tapping out a response.

As home circles became more popular, simple devices were manufactured to simplify the séance process. The rapping alphabet invented by the Fox sisters worked fine at first, but it had its limitations — it was time-consuming and tedious. Mediums and home circles started to use others writing techniques to speed up the process.

Instead of using a knocking system, participants of the home circle used a pencil basket to communicate with the spirit. A pencil basket consisted of a small basket with a pencil inserted into it to as a writing implement. Once the participant held the pencil basket in his hand the spirit would take over and use the pencil to write its message.

The pencil basket evolved into the heart-shaped planchette, a tool with rotating castors on each side and a hole at the tip where a pencil was inserted as the third leg. Like the pencil basket, the sitter held the planchette in his hand and let the spirit use it as a writing device. While the gadget moved freely and took less time than the knocking system or table tipping, many were frustrated by the writing techniques because the lettering was sloppy and mostly incoherent. Many got rid of the planchette altogether and opted to hold the pencil in their own hand, going into a trance-like state and letting the spirit communicate through their own body.

Alphabet Boards

While a trance worked for some sitters, there were many others who believed that one had to have the correct, precise equipment to effectively communicate with a ghost. Alphabet boards were manufactured for this purpose. An alphabet board consisted of a piece of wood that had the alphabet, the numbers 1-10, and useful phrases printed on it. The sitter used the board in conjunction with table tipping or pendulum as a quicker way to spell out messages.

Innovative spiritualists began to experiment with different ways to enhance the simple letter board. The invention of the dial plate telegraph made communication for the living more convenient. Many mediums surmised that if the telegraph was good enough for the living then it was good enough for the dead.

In 1853, spiritualist Isaac T. Pease invented the "Spiritual Telegraph Dial," which was a dial plate with the letters of the alphabet imprinted around its circumference. A needle was affixed to the dial so that it was spun to the appropriate letters to spell out the spirit's message.

With the success of Pease's dial plate, similar gadgets were manufactured and put on the market. The "Pytho" or "Thought Reader" was a round, stationary plate with letter and numbers around its circumference, a long needle swung back forth across the letters. Handles on each side of the board were hinged to the needle. A sitter on each side of the board held the handle in their hand and swung the needle to the appropriate letter or number.

In 1895, Milton Bradley made its own dial plate called "Genii, the Witches Fortune Teller," which consisted of two square pieces of oak wood sandwiched together. The top piece of wood had a hole cutout in the middle and the bottom piece had letters etched into it. The top piece of wood slid across the bottom piece stopping at the correct letters until the correct message was spelled out.

While dial plates had their purpose, many found their construction to be too cumbersome and impractical. Home circle participants began taking the dial plates apart, using the alphabet boards separately. Instead of the attached needle, a separate gliding point slid across the letters.

In the December 18, 1876, edition of the *American Spiritualist Magazine*, a letter about the alphabet board and gliding pointer technique started a phenomenon that turned into one of the most notorious devices for spirit communication. The letter's author, "LK," wrote:

"Many of your readers may wish to communicate with their spirit friends, but lack even that feeble mediumistic power which is generally considered the first step to or beginning of mediumistic development, viz: the power to communicate by tipping of the table. There has been discovered, by my wife, a method, which will enable many persons to get manifestations who could not get tippings of the table; and for those who require tipping of the table to point out the letters when the alphabet is called, a method is here offered that will facilitate operations greatly. My wife and myself, having discovered that we conjointly (not singly) were able to have intercourse with our spirit friends by tippings, found the process very tedious; but soon as we tried the new method our spirit son exclaimed: "Oh dear papa and mama you have made our work so easy now." The method is this: I have on the table painted the letters of the alphabet, thus: On this table we place a polished little rod, rounded below and pointed on both ends; The upper side is wide for the fingers to rest, and also rough so they do not glide off. The table of course must be very smooth—I facilitate operations by putting a little powdered soapstone on it. On this rod the fingers of the two persons sitting on the opposite sides are placed, and the rod is allowed to glide from letter to letter. With this little arrangement we receive messages now faster than by writing. If you think this information useful, your readers are welcome to it. Fraternally yours. LK"

With the popularity of the new technique came the need for a streamlined gliding pointer. Manufacturers dominated the market with a modernized heart-shaped planchette that no longer had the hole for a pencil. Instead, it sat on three legs with a hole in the middle to glide over the alphabet boards. Other manufacturers produced newer versions of the letter board that had a simpler placement of the alphabet and numbers to appropriate the use of the planchette.

Soon, entrepreneurs realized they could package the new planchette with an accompanying letter board and came up with the name "talking board" to call the new novelty item. Newspaper articles about the new talking board sensation were reprinted throughout the United States and Europe. As popularity thrived, other innovators put out their own version of the talking board to ride the lucrative wave of success. The talking board eventually became what we now know as the Ouija Board

The Ouija Board

In May 1890, Elijah Bond filed the first patent for the "Ouija Board," sighting Charles W. Kennard and William H. A. Maupin as the assigners. His patent was finally granted nearly a year later in February of 1892. Legend states the name "Ouija" came from a series of talking board sessions with Kennard. The spirit communicating with Kennard told him to name the board "Ouija" because it was Egyptian for "good luck." Incidentally, "Ouija" is not the Egyptian word for "good luck," still, the name stuck. It is unclear as to why it took so long for someone to mass-produce the Talking Board as a novelty item. However, the Ouija Board or "Egyptian Luck Board" became an instant hit.

Later, William Fuld gained the rights to the Ouija Board and, as part of his marketing strategy, revamped the history of the board. He said that he chose the name "Ouija" by merging together the French word "oui," meaning "yes', and the German word "ja," also meaning "yes." This became the first of many mythologies and superstitions about the Ouija Board. Fuld's company made Ouija Boards up until the rights were sold to Parker Brothers in 1966. Presently, they are still the manufactures of the modern-day Ouija Boards.

A OUIJA Board.

Skeptics Question Fox Sisters

As much as the Fox sisters were revered, they were just as equally scrutinized. Skeptics and critical reporters routinely attended the public performances denouncing the women as frauds. They claimed the sisters produced the knocking noises by cracking their toes, knee and ankle cracking, or the use of ventriloquism. Some even suggested that Maggie, Kate, and Leah were utilizing hidden mechanical devices to make the rapping sounds.

A series of committees were put together to test the three sisters more in hopes of exposing them as charlatans rather than to prove their authenticity. The girls were asked to perform a standard séance using their usual systematic knocking technique to communicate with the alleged spirit. As the members watched they would test out each practical plausible solution for the knockings until they found the real source of the trickery.

In the name of truth, the committee members, mostly men, were ruthless with their investigation of the Fox sisters and spared no prudence that would normally be implemented to the fairer sex. Many times the women were subjected to what they deemed to be embarrassing tests that made them feel vulnerable and manhandled.

In some instances their feet or knees were bound to make sure that the three women were not cracking their bones in order to make the knocking sounds. Other times the sisters were asked to stand on chairs and hold up their skirts so that the viewers could make sure they weren't making the noises with their knees or any other portion of their body.

Especially Kate and Maggie were emotionally ruffled by the rueful analysis of their body and undergarments. Both girls would often break down into crying fits after the tests complaining that the committees were disrespectful and indecent in their poking and prodding. They were not used to such public scrutiny and didn't understand why they were focused on with such great detailed attention.

Though the three sisters disliked and even despised the rigorous testing, they went through it anyway to prove that they were, in fact, genuine. They knew that if the committee were never able to find anything that it would prove to the skeptics and disbelievers that they weren't tricking the public to make a fast buck.

In the end, even with the strictest testing methods, no committee was ever able to figure out a plausible way the Fox sisters were able to make the knocking noises. However, they did find there seemed to be some inconsistencies with the answers to duplicate questions. Many times, if the same question was asked a second time, the answer would be different — a peculiarity that was never explained.

Unfortunately, though the Fox sisters complied with all of the intrusive testing and were even cleared of the forgery of the knocking noises, their every move still seemed to be under a microscope. Leah was often accused of priming the séances by gleaning information about their prospective clients beforehand to ensure a successful spirit interaction. This suspicion came into play because the three sisters only scheduled their sittings in advance and would not perform without at least twenty-four hours notice.

Other inconsistencies in their practices attracted negative commentary. Kate, Maggie, and Leah were often able to call upon the dead famous, but could not conjure up impressive, accurate results. At one particularly embarrassing sitting, Benjamin Franklin's spirit came through only to have trouble spelling and lacking the basics of grammar. When viewers of the séance critiqued the horrid spelling, Maggie took it very personally and stormed off, bellowing that she was never good at grammar.

Still, even with the inconsistencies, there were many who believed that the Fox sisters were the real thing. For as much criticism as the three women received it never seemed to affect their thriving fan base. Though, eventually, the pressure of fame took its toll crippling Kate and Maggie Fox for the rest of their lives. They were thrown off their pedestal by their own accord and not by their many critics who tried to push them off. In the end they died destitute and penniless.

The Fall of the Fox Sisters

Maggie Fox stopped performing séances to be a bride. She fell in love with the well-known aristocrat and Arctic explorer, Elisha Kent Kane, whom she had met while touring through Philadelphia. Kane was instantly attracted to Maggie, but did not like that she was a medium. Later, after getting to know the family dynamics between the three sisters, he announced that he was sure both Maggie and Kate were frauds. Even worse they were being controlled and manipulated by Leah to keep the lucrative amounts of money coming in. He persuaded Maggie to leave the medium circuit to be with him.

Even though Kane and Maggie were smitten for each other, there were other issues to consider. Kane's parents did not approve of Maggie because of her middle-class upbringing. They adamantly stated that the family would never accept the idea of Maggie and Elisha as a couple and discouraged marriage altogether. Kane respected his parents' wishes and never properly married Maggie. However, the couple did have a private commitment ceremony exchanging vows and rings in front of their closest (and accepting) friends and family, but happiness it seemed would elude Maggie and Elisha. Soon after their commitment ceremony, tragedy struck the couple. During his travels Kane developed scurvy and never completely recovered. He died in 1857 from complications of the deadly illness.

Left heart-broken and penniless, Maggie ventured into the world of séances to make ends meet. She never fully emotionally recovered from the blow of Kent's death. This was made worst by the fact that rumors were spread that she was never truly married to Kent. Wrenched with pain, she vehemently declared that she was his one and only true wife, a statement she could not prove because she was not legally bound to Kent and therefore could not inherit any of his assets. The stress became too much and Maggie took up drinking to settle her nerves.

Kate did not fare a much better plight. She too, started to drink alcohol heavily, and it often wreaked havoc on her sittings. Steadily, her reputation declined as a pathetic drunk. In 1871, Kate seemed to rejuvenate some of her old wit and traveled to England to perform a series of performances with a number of well-known British Spiritualists. She remained in England for a year and met a barrister name Henry Jecken. Their engagement was brief and shortly they married.

From her marriage to Jecken, Kate had two sons who were reported to have inherited the same gifts that she displayed. Her first son, Ferdinand, was said to have mediumistic abilities by the time he was three years old and rumors stated that while spirits channeled through his body he would radiate with an unearthly glow.

By 1885, the Spiritualism Movement declined at a rapid state. Many of the mediums working the circuits were denounced as frauds once again putting the light on Maggie. She was interrogated and tested by a New York commission and this time Maggie failed the inquiry. She was deemed a charlatan and her sterling reputation had finally been tarnished.

Still in England, Kate was not spared her share of tragedy. In 1888, her husband died of a stroke. Depressed and emotionally wrought, Kate took her comfort from the bottle. Her drunken states were so out of control that her two boys were taken into custody by welfare workers. They went to live with an uncle in England, by the hands of Maggie, who was able to make sure that the two boys were, at least, raised by family.

In the same year, Maggie made a statement that changed the plight of Spiritualism forever. She booked a performance at the New York Academy of Music, walked on-stage, and confessed that she and Kate were frauds. She explained that the pair had made the knocking and rapping sounds at the Hydesville cottage by cracking their toes and using an apple.

"When we went to bed at night, we used to tie an apple to a string and move the string up and down, causing the apple to bump on the floor, or we would drop the apple on the floor, making a strange noise every time it would rebound. Mother listened to this for a time. She would not understand it and did not suspect us as being capable of a trick because we were so young," Maggie said.

She went on to say that their older sister Leah had forced them into publicly performing séances because of the money. Kate sat in a box above the stage silently. She neither confirmed nor denied her sister's claims.

In a written confession published in the October 21, 1888, edition of *The New York World Newspaper*, Maggie expounded on her career as a fraudulent medium and how she and her sister were taught to make the raps and knocks.

> "Mrs. Underhill [Leah] my eldest sister took Katie and me to Rochester. There it was that we discovered a new way to make the raps. My sister Katie was the first to observe that by swishing her fingers she could produce certain noises with her knuckles and joints, and that the same effect could be made with the toes. Finding that we could make raps with our feet — first with one foot and then with both — we practiced until we could do this easily when the room was dark. Like most perplexing things when made clear, it is astonishing how easily it is done. The rapping are simply the result of a perfect control of the muscles of the leg below the knee, which govern the tendons of the foot and allow action of the toe and ankle bones that is not commonly known. Such perfect control is only possible when the child is taken at an early age and carefully and continually taught to practice the muscles, which grow stiffer in later years. ... This, then, is the simple explanation of the whole method of the knocks and raps...
>
> "A great many people, when they hear the rapping, imagine at once that the spirits are touching them. It is a very common delusion. Some very wealthy people came to see me some years ago when I lived in Forty-Second Street and I did some rappings for them. I made the spirit rap on the chair and one of the ladies cried out: 'I feel the spirit tapping me on the shoulder.' Of course that was pure imagination."

The critics reveled in Maggie's confession while her devoted fan base was skeptic of it. They cited that it was the rant of a lonely and tired, drunk but did not refute the idea of Spiritualism. Later, Kate publicly denounced her sister's confession and continued to perform as a medium.

Three years later, Maggie recanted her own confession, explaining that the announcement was made in spite to get back at their sister, Leah, who they felt had used them to make a fortune. Both Kate and Maggie grew to despise Leah, who had since married a wealthy businessman. Leah thought of her two sisters as an embarrassment, cutting ties with them and taking a large portion of the fortune from prior years of performances and private sittings.

In 1892, Kate died of alcohol poisoning. Only 56 years old, she was found by one of her sons. Maggie died a year later at the age of 59 at a friend's home in Brooklyn. Both women were in poverty at the time of their death. They were buried in pauper's graves.

The Aftermath

After the deaths of Kate and Maggie, the Fox family was once again put under intense scrutiny. There was never any proof that the Hydesville cottage was the scene of a murder. Many speculated that the girls knew of the rumors about the peddler's death and exploited it for profit.

However, a turn of events in 1904 would change speculation into evidence. The Hydesville cottage had been deserted and dilapidated for some time. Only parts of the house remained in tattered pieces. One day, a group of local kids were playing in the ruins. The east wall of the cellar collapsed nearly trapping and killing one of boys. A man who came to their aid realized that the flimsy wall had been a false partition. That's why it had fallen so easily. There between the false partition and the true wall of the cellar he found a crumbling corpse of man and a tin that had the name "Charles B. Rosma" inscribed in it. Upon examination he realized that a portion of the man's skull was missing. John Fox had found a piece of bone fragment when he had dug up the cellar. Everything seemed to be finally coming into place.

Were the bones remnants of the missing peddler? Did he haunt the Hydesville cottage and communicate with the Fox sisters? There have been many speculations and claims, but no one will ever know. By the time the body was found, most of the Fox family was dead and buried. Perhaps, if Kate and Maggie had not drunk themselves to death, they could have been vindicated in life. Instead they died masked in a shroud of question, disbelief, and suspicion. We will never know if they were authentic mediums or just clever children.

Daniel Douglas Home

The Incredible Flying Man

Considered to be one of the most gifted and powerful mediums of the time, Daniel Douglas Home (pronounced "Hume") was also considered to be one of the most pretentious and aloof. He was known not to affiliate with other mediums of the time because he felt he had nothing to learn from them. He considered them charlatans who could not compete with his natural all-powerful mediumistic abilities.

Born on March 20, 1833, in Edinburgh, Scotland, Home immediately began to show signs of psychic abilities. His crib would move back and forth on its own accord like phantom hands were lulling the baby to sleep. By the age of four, Home accurately predicted his cousin's death. Aside from the "curse" of second sight, the boy showed idiosyncrasies including a nervous temperament. He was thin, pale, and often sick.

Since she had other children, Elizabeth, decided that she did not have the patience or the time to deal with the boy's strange behavior. Home was shuffled off to his childless aunt, Mary Cook, and her husband, who lived in Portobello, a small coastal town three miles away from Edinburgh. She took the boy in and treated him like her own.

Within a few years, the Cooks immigrated to the United States taking a ship to New York and then traveling to Greenville, Connecticut. In the new land, Home's bouts of illness increased to the point where it was almost impossible for him to play with his fellow schoolmates. Instead, he took to staying indoors and reading the Bible.

Eventually, Home befriended a boy named Edwin who was also sickly. The pair spent their time walking in the woods, reading scripture together, and discussing their mortality. Home believed that the deceased were all around him making their presence known and communicating with him. Intrigued by the phenomenon, the two boys made a promise that whoever died first would contact the other from the afterlife.

However, the friendship was short-lived because the Cooks moved 150 miles away to Troy, New York. With a good amount of distance between them, Home and Edwin lost contact with each other but neither forgot their pact. One night the boy was awoken from sleep by a bright light at the foot of his bed. Upon closer examination, Home realized that the light was actually the outline of a figure that looked similar to his childhood friend. Edwin raised his hand and traced three circles in the air then disappeared. Home took the vision as a sign that Edwin had died and was holding up his end of the pact. A short time later the boy received a letter explaining that his childhood friend had died of malignant dysentery exactly three days before he had the vision. Home realized that Edwin was drawing three circles in the air to signify his time of death.

Daniel Douglas Home, 1852.
Public Domain.

This was not the last time Home correctly predicted the time of death of someone close to him. A few years later, the Cooks moved back to Greenville, Connecticut. Home's birth mother emigrated from Scotland to be closer to her family who had moved to Waterford just a few miles outside of Greenville. Home was happy to be reunited with his mom, but the reconciliation was short-lived. In 1850, the boy saw a vision of his mother saying, "Dan, twelve o'clock." Shortly afterward his mother died at precisely 12:00 in the afternoon.

By the time Home turned fifteen the presence of his sixth sense began to take on other forms. Rapping and knocking noises plagued the Cook home. Tables vibrated and objects moved. Home's aunt was so distressed by the new phenomenon she invited a series of ministers to identify the source of the activity. While Home thought the paranormal phenomenon was a sign that God existed, Cook and her visiting clergyman believed that the knockings were the work of the Devil. It was determined that the way to get rid of the presence of the Devil was to get rid of the source. Home was considered the source and his aunt kicked him out of the house.

During the same time, the Fox Sisters had just hit fame and were traveling larger cities showcasing their medium performances to packed theaters. Home took notice and, as a way of survival, he performed his own séances in return for gifts, food, and lodging. By the time Home turned eighteen, he had become widely successful. In 1851, one of his sittings was written up in a Hartford newspaper and his fame flourished overnight.

Home performed séances in a different way that set him apart from most mediums. He took care to study other sittings by prominent spiritualists and deemed most of them scoundrels. Home believed that his gifts were natural born and he had no need for the usual cunning and trickery other mediums used.

To distinguish himself, Home performed his séances in a brightly lit room. He used lettered cards to spell out the messages the spirits were communicating to him. Phantom hands ending at the wrist materialized from thin air and shook hands with each of the participants. Tables vibrated and objects moved. Disembodied music played. Sometimes Home's body would shrink or become larger. To further his believability, he had the sitters hold his hands and legs while the phenomenon appeared.

Even with the lights on and the amazing evidence he was able to materialize, nothing surpassed his most amazing feat. During a séance in Connecticut at the home of successful silk manufacturer, Ward Cheney, Home allegedly levitated twice in the air hitting the ceiling. The table moved and vibrated thrashing about with a sound that some compared to a storm at sea.

Present at the séance was journalist, F. L. Burr, who was assigned to debunk Home and the Spiritualism movement in general. However, instead of writing a scathing review, he wrote:

> "Suddenly, without any expectation on the part of the company, Home was taken up into the air. I had hold of his hand at the time and I felt his feet — they were lifted a foot from the floor. He palpitated from head to foot with the contending emotions of joy and fear, which choked his utterances. Again and again, he was taken from the floor, and the third time he was taken to the ceiling of the apartment, with which his hands and feet came into gentle contact."

After the article came out (and was republished many times), Home became so famous that at the pinnacle of his success he was performing up to six or seven séances a day. He was favored especially in the city of New York and took residence in Bryant Park on 42nd Street.

In 1855, word of Home's amazing levitation abilities traveled across the Atlantic Ocean and he was invited to tour through Europe to perform séances. With Home suffering from the side-effects of tuberculosis, a friend suggested to him that the air in Europe would help him recuperate, which prompted Home to make the trip. Home took a ship to England and lodged at a large hotel in London owned by William Cox. The entrepreneur was a believer in spiritualism and knew of Home's reputation. He was so enamored with the idea of Home staying in his hotel that he let the medium lodge in a room for free.

During his stay in Europe, Home only catered to wealthy and famous patrons, including Napoleon III, Queen Sophia of The Netherlands, and Robert and Elizabeth Barrett Browning. Robert despised Home's antics and wrote an unfavorable poem called, "Mr. Sludge, The Medium" about his experience. His wife, however, believed Home to be a true authentic medium and it became a bone of contention between the couple.

In 1866, Home's sterling reputation was tarnished by a scandalous court case involving a wealthy widow. Mrs. Lyon took Home into her house and treated him as an adopted son. In her claims she stated that she gave the medium 60,000 pounds to gain her entrance into high society. However, when her affiliation with Home did not help her reputation she demanded the money back.

Home countered her accusations and declared that the money was given freely for his medium and spiritual services. It was only when he denied Mrs. Lyon's sexual advances that she asked for her money back. The burden of proof was on Home and since he had no circumstantial evidence to substantiate his claim the court ruled against him and he was forced to return the money to the widow.

Despite the outcome of the court case, Home's supporters believed that he held himself with the utmost respect and acted as a true gentleman. Though he was heavily publicly scrutinized, his patrons stuck by his side.

Around the time of the trial, Home's abilities were increasingly growing until at one séance he performed his most memorable feat. In December 1886, the medium was the guest of one of his best friends, Lord Adare, who would later become the Fourth Earl of Dunraven. Adare was fascinated with Home's abilities and for a year had documented his sittings. It was at his house that the medium was said to fall into a deep trance and then lift off the ground, floating through a third floor window and into another window landing in an adjacent room. This amazing feat was witnessed by three of London's most important high society, including Lord Adare himself, his cousin Captain Charles Wynne, and the Master of Lindsay.

Though skeptics tried to denounce his levitation as fraud, his viewers had such good reputations it was hard to sway the public. Unlike the public scrutiny and rigorous testing the Fox Sisters had to endure, Home never had to go under any testing that even came close. His reputation and standing with the rich and famous and his poor health seemed to buffer him from anything more than skeptical reviews that were never founded with any sort of fact.

In 1873, at the age of 38, Home retired from the medium circuit citing that he was in poor health and his abilities were beginning to wane. He died June 21, 1886 from complications of tuberculosis. He is buried in the St. Germain-en-Laye cemetery.

Sir Arthur Conan Doyle 1890. *Public Domain.*

Sir Arthur Conan Doyle

Spirit Photography

Arthur Conan Doyle was born May 22, 1859, in Edinburgh, Scotland. His father, Charles Doyle, worked as an assistant surveyor. He was an epileptic and an alcoholic, which made it hard for him to deal with the consistency and tedium of his position. In his 40s he left his job and spent the duration of his life in sanitariums and nursing homes for alcoholics.

Doyle's mother, Mary, was the consistent parent in the household. She had ten children, seven that survived: two boys and five girls. She was an avid reader and a natural storyteller. Later in life, Doyle would cite his mother as the key inspiration for his love of writing.

During his school years, Doyle was able to attend a Catholic institution for free hoping that he would dedicate his life to the Church. However, he soon realized that it was not his calling and he decided to go to medical school instead. His family did not have the financial needs to pay for his tuition, so Doyle worked part-time jobs while he attended college. In 1881, he completed a Bachelor's in Medicine after attending for five years.

After college, Doyle's goal was to start his own private practice. As a way to make ends meet while he worked on getting regular clients, he wrote short stories and sold them to magazines. In 1886, Doyle wrote his first Sherlock Holmes story called, "A Study in Scarlet," but had a difficult time selling it. Eventually, he sold it to *Beeton's Christmas Annual* for a small sum and it was published over a year later.

By the time the story was published, Doyle had grown out of the idea of writing detective short stories. Instead, he wrote an historical novel called *Micah Clarke* that was published in 1889. The book was an instant success and Doyle used it as a springboard to write six more Sherlock Holmes stories that were published in a brand new magazine called *Strand*. The short stories were widely received and an American publisher contacted Doyle to write a full-length Sherlock Holmes novel. He fulfilled his contract and wrote the book, *The Sign of the Four*.

Doyle thought of himself as a serious author. He decided he did not want to write more series novels and pursued other options. He began writing another historical novel, *The White Company*, which he thought was his best work to date. However, the character Sherlock Holmes had such an outstanding readership that the publisher offered Doyle increasingly lucrative sums of money for each story written. Doyle finally relented to his following and kept up writing Sherlock Holmes novels as a supplement income to his medical practice, which he considered his official career.

During the next few years Doyle struggled with his medical practice. He even considered specializing in eye care and attended a six-month training course in Vienna. The trip was short-lived by circumstance and frustration. The lectures were taught in German which Doyle only had a conversational grasp. He did not understand many of the technical terms and was lost in the language.

Defeated, Doyle returned to England and settled in London in Devonshire Place. He began the uphill task of trying to reclaim his meager medical practice. However, his house was located in a remote location that was impractical for what he was trying to accomplish. With the long hours of waiting, Doyle had plenty of time to write and he wrote more of his accomplished Sherlock Holmes stories. The tales became an instant success and the medical doctor decided to close his practice for good and accept the idea of being a full-time writer.

As soon as Doyle put all of his energies into writing, his success grew to that of celebrity. He captured two markets: those who knew him from the popular Sherlock Holmes mysteries and those who knew him from his best-selling adventure books. This gave him more notoriety than most writers of the time and he was highly respected because of his participation in public affairs. Doyle was an avid sportsman and outdoorsman. He boxed, played soccer, and cricket, which gave him a reputation for being not only a gifted intellectual, but also a robust man's man.

Since he had long ago given up the Catholic faith, Doyle searched for spirituality in other areas. He participated in séances and experiments dealing with telepathy and transference. His fascination with psychic phenomenon led him to join The Psychical Research Society in 1893. Like many who were well-educated and in high standing, his interest at first was based in skepticism, as he hoped to find a way to explain what others considered unexplainable. However, the experiences of his own life would change his way of thinking forever.

Doyle's wife, Louise, suffered with a long bout of tuberculosis; the writer became fiercely obsessed with finding a cure and ignored other doctors who explained to him that she only had a few more months to live. Determined to keep his wife alive, Doyle put aside his career and focused primarily on finding a treatment for consumption. The couple, along with their daughter, Mary, and his son, Kingsley, traveled to Switzerland and later returned to England in the county of Surrey. A fellow writer, Grant Allen, who also suffered from tuberculosis, suggested the countryside's climate and air had benefited his disease easing the symptoms. Doyle bought a large house in the area that had top-notch amenities including the new addition of electricity. He and his family stayed at the home until 1906 when his wife died.

A year later, Doyle married another woman, Jean Leckie, whom he had met while his wife convalesced with her illness. He did not have an affair with the woman (though it was highly speculated) who was fourteen years younger than him, but instead stayed faithful to wife until the very end. Shortly after his first wife's death, the relationship with Jean turned romantic and during their marriage she had three more children.

After the grief of losing his first wife had whittled away, Doyle regained his active life in public affairs. He joined societies, went to dinner parties and maintained a spot in the limelight. The writer traveled to the United States performing book signings and public speaking events. The Sherlock Holmes mysteries were just as popular in America and Doyle was well-received. People loved his Scottish accent and his quick intellect.

Doyle had a passionate side to him that sometimes fueled an obligation. When his first wife was alive his passion drove him to do anything to find a cure for consumption to save her life. With that same focused intent, when the Boer War broke out, he was compelled to volunteer in South Africa. He stayed there for three months and stirred up controversy. Many heckled Doyle explaining that he took his fiction character, Sherlock Holmes, too seriously by trying to become him.

The writer took it in stride and when he returned he decided to get into politics. In 1900, Doyle ran for Parliament in the general election. He was a Conservative candidate for the Unionist party who were pro-military. The writer made speeches on the streets and formal presentations in theaters. Despite his eloquence, Doyle lost the race because his views were considered to be too conservative for the Surrey area, which held a more liberal stance on politics. Later, Doyle would admit that he was glad that he lost because he felt that he probably would not have been a good politician. Still, he stayed active in political issues. In 1902, the writer was knighted and became officially known as Sir Author Conan Doyle.

In 1917, Doyle campaigned for the Spiritualism movement by lecturing throughout Britain. His presentations were widely received and he spoke to a packed house. He suspected that part of his popularity was due to his famous reputation as the man who invented Sherlock Holmes. Still, he didn't care because he knew that he had an attentive audience. If his fame brought the people to his lectures his ideas were, at least, being heard and perhaps being taken seriously. Doyle's presentations became so popular that he took his tour to Europe, the United States, Australia and Africa.

In 1918, Doyle's only son, Kingsley, died of pneumonia and then, coincidentally, a few weeks later, his brother, Innes, also died of pneumonia. The writer fell into a deep depression and looked to Spiritualism for answers. He participated in séances hoping to get into contact with his deceased son. During a séance with a Welsh medium Doyle was sure he heard the voice of Kingsley coming through from the other side.

Two years later, when his mother died, Doyle sat with William and Eva Thompson, two mediums from the United States. During that séance, the writer was convinced he witnessed the materialized apparition of his dead mother. However, days later the mediums were arrested as frauds when police officers found costume make-up and wigs in their personal possessions.

Despite the arrest, Doyle held fast to his belief that he saw his mother. He was criticized harshly for his acceptance of spirit communication. Many wondered how a man who wrote crime mysteries about "Sherlock Holmes," a character that used intellect and logic to solve cases, could believe so fiercely into something as illogical as communication with the deceased. The critics never swayed Doyle, who was resolute in his spiritual path, and began to see at as part of his life's work. During the 1920s he spent over a quarter of a million pounds advancing the Spiritualism movement through speaking presentations, hosting séances and writing books. In 1926, Doyle wrote a spiritual adventure book call, *The Land of Mist*. During the same time period he also wrote, *The History of Spiritualism*, a two-volume set that chronicled the lives of many mediums including the Fox Sisters.

Doyle also performed paranormal investigations. In Dorset, he investigated a haunted house that he chronicled in the book, *On the Edge of the Unknown*. In a weird twist, after the investigation, the house burned down. During the excavation, a child's body was found buried in the garden. Once the body was exhumed and taken from the property, the paranormal activity seemed to disappear. Doyle speculated that the child was responsible for the haunting and when his body was found there was no need to haunt the location anymore.

The Cottingley Fairies

In 1920, Doyle was commissioned by *Strand Magazine* to write an article on fairies. Through his fellow Spiritualist friend, Felicia Scatcher, he had heard of two prints taken in 1917 that were proof of fairies; the photos were taken by two girls in the Cottingley area.

Doyle was in contact with Theosophist, Edward Gardner, who had in his possession the two photos in question. He borrowed the prints which one showed 10-year-old, Frances Griffiths, surrounded by a group of tiny dancing women with clear wings. The second picture depicted sixteen-year-old Elsie White sitting on the grass shaking hands with a miniature gnome.

Cottingley Fairies Photo #1. *Public Domain*.

Instantly, Doyle believed in the phenomenon and showed the pictures to psychical researcher, Sir Oliver Lodge, who claimed they were faked. He even had a clairvoyant psychic perform psychometry on the pictures for impressions. Unfortunately, she didn't come up with anything circumstantial.

Doyle took the criticism in stride, but was headstrong about his belief in the fairy pictures. He sent Gardner to Cottingley to speak to the family in person to get a feel for their character. In Cottingley, Gardner found out the pictures were taken by White and Griffiths, the two girls in the pictures. They claimed they had been playing together in the garden area and spotted the cluster of fairies. Vowing to get pictures of the small creatures White borrowed her father's camera and waited until they appeared.

Upon Gardner's return, he stated that the girls and their parents seemed honest and respectful. Doyle took this as the proof he needed to show that the fairy photographs were, indeed, real. However, a little skepticism did creep in. He and Gardner decided to send White and Griffiths twenty photographic plates to take more pictures of the fairies in the Cottingley woods. If the girls sent back more original pictures with fairies in then that meant that the phenomenon was genuine without a doubt.

While waiting for the other photos, Doyle published the two original photos along with his article on fairies. He used aliases for the family and the two girls to protect their identity. The article was published in November 1920 and sold out a few short weeks of its publication. The Cottingley fairies were widely debated and much speculation surfaced as to how to they were faked. Along with Doyle, there were many who argued that the pictures were positive proof of spiritual phenomenon.

The newspaper, *The Westminister Gazette*, broke the code for the alias Doyle used for the White family. They sent a reporter to talk to the two girls to garner any misinformation or facts left out of the article in *Strand Magazine*. The reporter found that all accounts by Doyle were correct. Also, he explained that the White family was very open and truthful. Nothing more was added to the story and the photos were officially pronounced as unexplained.

In 1921, White traveled to London to hand off the new photographs to Doyle. There three additional photos that showed interaction with fairies. Gardner and the writer were ecstatic to have three new photos of the girls interacting with fairies and founded their belief with absolute proof. Doyle took the three photos and printed them in *Strand Magazine* with and additional article on other sightings and encounters with fairies.

The new article, once again, created controversy, but this time readers were more critical of the new photographs. They criticized that the pictures were sharpened like a professional photographer had taken them. Also, the hairstyles and clothing seemed too modern and too fashionable to be true fairies.

The new article spurred clairvoyant, Geoffrey Hodson, to visit the White family in Cottingley to witness the fairies to verify their authenticity. Hodson met with Elsie White and she took him to the forest where she spotted the fairy. No pictures were taken of the trip, but Hodson later reported that he witnessed the fairies first-hand. This was the proof that most people needed to authenticate the photos and Doyle's articles.

The writer used the momentum from the second article as inspiration for his next book, *The Coming of the Fairies*, which was published a year later. In the new book, Doyle was particularly enamored with the fifth and final picture in the Cottingley fairies series. It depicted the back of the two fairies standing side-by-side. The writer explained:

> "Seated on the upper left hand edge with wing well displayed is an undraped fairy apparently considering whether it is time to get up. An earlier riser of more mature age is seen on the right possessing abundant hair and wonderful wings. Her slightly denser body can be glimpsed within her fairy dress."

Elsie White stayed out of the limelight for over fifty years until 1971 when the BBC channel in England interviewed her for a follow-up piece. A reporter interviewed White for ten days and even traveled back to the Cottingley location where the fairy photographs were taken. Elsie was asked outright if she and Frances had faked the pictures. She stated that she'd rather not say leaving some to believe that her ambiguous answer was the same as admitting to a hoax.

Both Francis and Elsie were again interviewed in 1976, but outright refuted the idea that the pictures were fakes. However, in 1981, Joe Cooper interviewed the two women for an article in *The Unexplained Magazine*. In the interview the cousins admitted that the first four pictures were faked. They used cutouts and hatpins to stage the photographs. However, with the confession they also vehemently stated that there were true fairies in the garden area and the fifth picture was, in fact, real.

William Hope and the Crewe Circle

Spirit photography was one of Doyle's passions and he collected as many pictures of reported phenomenon as he could find. He was an active participant in the Crew Circle (named after the city, Crewe), a group lead by William Hope whose purpose was to manifest spirit photography.

Hope had been working with spirit photography since 1905 when he took a picture of a friend that just happened to have the silhouette of an extra person in it. The figure turned out to be the deceased sister of the photo subject.

From there, Hope took his new found passion for spirit photography and eventually founded the Crewe Circle for like-minded Spiritualists who had an interest in spirit photography. In the beginning the group was discreet staying under the radar to keep unwanted attention. They took pictures and then destroyed the negatives for fear that they would be accused of witchcraft. However, when Archbishop Thomas Colley — and advocate for the supernatural — joined the group, their work went public.

With the newfound publicity came the usual scrutiny. Hope was accused of being a fraud and that his pictures were doctored to show the spirit "extras" that prominently displayed themselves. By this time Hope had moved to London and had become a prominent and successful medium in the Spiritualism movement, so it was inevitable that his methods would be questioned.

As a preventive measure Hope put together a system to rule out any kind of fraud. He used a plate camera that was in plain sight and could be examined at will. Sitters brought their own sealed plates. When the package was opened the subject was required to sign or initial the plate so that it would appear on the picture. Furthermore, the sitter was to take the plate out of the camera and follow Hope into the darkroom to watch the photo development process.

In this picture an alleged spirit is manifesting over the group at the annual meeting of the "Society for the Study of Supernormal Pictures." Sir Arthur Conan Doyle is in the middle with his wife to the left. 1922. *Public Domain*.

Harry Price

In February 1922, Harry Price, a magician and paranormal investigator, made it a point to test Hope and his method for producing spirit "extras" in his photos. At this time Price had just joined The Society for Psychical Research (SPR) and did not have the reputation as a leading ghost hunter that he would later in his career. However, even in the short time as a member of the Society, he already exposed a good amount of mediums as charlatans.

Price participated in a séance with Hope, but did not follow the fail-proof procedures verbatim. He brought his own photo plates, but after the picture was taken he refused to sign it. While Hope was preoccupied, Price tampered with the mediums own photographic slides. He punctured them with twelve needle holes to see if the medium would change Price's plates for his own. To further the control Price's own pack of photographic plates were imprinted with the Imperial Dry Plate Co. logo. If Price's plates were used then the company's trademark would show up on the negative. He joined Hope in the darkroom and watched carefully has the medium developed his picture. At one point Price thought he saw Hope slip his negative in this breast pocket and pull out a different one.

After the photograph was developed by the medium, Price studied the print searching for his twelve puncture marks or the logo imprint. Neither was present. This could only mean one thing; Hope had switched the actual slide. Price did not accuse the medium as a fraud or show any contempt. Nor did he mention that he thought he saw the slight-of-hand switch of the photograph's slide. Instead, he wrote about the incident in the May issue of the *Journal of the London Society of Psychical Research*. The article, "Cold Light on Spiritualistic Phenomena," chronicled Price's experience and denounced Hope as a fraud. Later the article was published as a separate booklet and circulated.

Doyle, a regular member of the Crewe Circle and a devout believer in the spirit photography phenomenon immediately defended Hope and his methods. He waged a personal war against Price and his tactics. In writing, he accused Price of switching the plates himself to discredit the medium and the Spiritualism movement in general. Doyle took great measures to try and clear Hope's name even going so far as to write a book called, *The Case of Spirit Photography*.

More than a decade after the incident with Price, a widow of one of Hope's assistants confessed in an article that there may have been trickery involved with the spirit photographs. She stated that after Hope's séance with Price her husband had "found in a suitcase a flash lamp with a bulb attachment, some cutout photographic heads, and some hairs."

Harry Price. 1932. *Public Domain*.

A photo of Harry Price with a spirit "extra" taken by William Hope. 1922. *Public Domain*.

Over the years, Hope was accused of fraud many times. However, there were many instances where respectable witnesses claimed that without a doubt that his spirit photographs were real. Doyle never wavered and stayed true to Hope and the Crewe Circle.

Doyle's Final Days

In the 1920s, Doyle suffered from a series of small heart attacks. Doctors warned that the stress of traveling and speaking would catch up with him if he didn't stop pushing himself so hard. However, Doyle was an adventurous soul and ignored the doctor's request explaining that he still had too much to do. By the spring of 1930 his health finally deteriorated and he was diagnosed with heart disease. In July, he caught a cold while lecturing in Scandinavia. He was sent home and put on bed rest. On July 7, 1930, surrounded by family and friends, Doyle died of a heart attack at the age of 71.

Early Paranormal Investigators

The Spiritualism movement literally created a need for paranormal investigations. As spirit communication became more popular so did fraud. Most took mediums at face value and believed their claims of communicating with the deceased. Charlatans used conjuring and other mentalist techniques to manifest "spirits," ectoplasm, disembodied appendages and ghostly music. They traveled from town to town staying just long to enough to make a splash, collect the profits and move on to the next settlement. There were those who were legitimate mediums and believed whole-heartedly in the movement. They provided their services with the best of intentions and because they genuinely wanted to help others with their mediumistic abilities. However, those who believed in spirit communication did so with a reverent faith that warranted very little evidence, so there was no differentiation between genuine mediums and scoundrels.

As a result, many scientists and other professionals took it upon themselves to study the growing phenomenon. They scrutinized mediums and their techniques, exposing frauds and giving credibility to those whose methods could not be explained. Paranormal researchers were hated among the spiritualist community and soon there was a divide between those who were faith-based and those who wanted more scientific evidence.

Many investigators were magicians who tried to inform the public of medium trickery through magic demonstrations. Harry Houdini spent his entire life going to séances and denouncing mediums by exposing their methods. He and Sir Arthur Conan Doyle became fast friends but inevitably their staunch opposite views of spiritualism would ruin their friendship forever.

The famous medium team, the Davenport Brothers, started their careers as magicians who, using some of the more well-known mediums, conjured tricks in their performances. However, their act was almost too good. Audience members proclaimed them as true mediums and they spent the rest of their careers performing séances.

However, many researchers started their careers as skeptics and through their experiences inevitably became convinced of the phenomenon even though their reputations were tarnished, scrutinized, or discredited.

Sir William Crookes

Sir William Crookes, a chemist and physicist, was later discredited for his involvement in Spiritualism. He discovered the element, thallium, and its correct atomic weight. In 1859, Crookes founded *Chemist News*, a science magazine he edited most of his life. Later, in 1864, he founded the *Quarterly Journal of Science* and was well respected as a scientist.

However, in 1867 his youngest brother died. The two were very close and, like many other grieving souls, he took his solace in spirit communication. Crooke's first participation in a séance was with Daniel Douglas Home. He was so impressed by the manifested phenomenon that he wanted to see if he could recreate it in a lab setting. Despite being able to recreate some of the phenomenon in a laboratory, he devised a theory that Home had a "physical force" around his body that emanated and helped contact with the spirits. He wrote a paper on the findings that were heavily criticized by his peers.

Crookes took the scrutiny in stride and continued his experiments with other mediums. Next, he worked with Florence Cook who had a spirit guide who regularly manifested by the name Katie King. In a four-month series of investigations at his home laboratory, Crookes aimed to prove that Cook and King were indeed two separate entities; the one being a live person while the other was a spirit manifestation.

He took a slurry of pictures of both Cook and King stating that the spirit was prettier and four inches tall than her live counterpart. Also, Cook had pierced ears while King did not. Crookes even managed to take pictures of Cook in a trance state with King showing herself in a full-body apparition.

Crookes conducted séances with Cook where she was tied up safely in her spirit cabinet. King would show herself and, in one instance, took part in being weighed and measured by the participants. Many scrutinized Cook's séances proclaiming that book Cook and King resembled each other in build and facial features. However, Crookes and other believers suggested that the resemblance was only because Cook used her own energies to manifest the spirit and therefore took on some of her features.

Crookes findings from his experiments with Cook were, again, largely scrutinized, this time to the point where he almost lost his membership in the Fellowship of Royal Society. With his reputation in the balance, Crookes stopped publicly publishing or talking of his involvement in the spiritualism movement until he was no longer under the microscope. In 1874, he once again published an article stating that he believed in mediumship and spirit communication. However, he did not immerse himself in anymore experiments. Instead he went back to conducting chemistry experiments; as a result, he was instrumental in the invention of vacuum tubes and cathode rays.

Sir William Crookes. 1904. *Public Domain.*

The Society of Psychical Research

In 1882, The Society for Psychical Research was founded to investigate fraudulent mediums, séances, spirit photography, and other means of spirit communication. It was considered the first group dedicated to the study of the paranormal through scientific means. Members included many prominent celebrities and scientists including Edmund Gurney, Henry Sedgwick, Frederick Myers, Lewis Carroll, Mark Twain and William Gladstone. Harry Price, Sir Arthur Conan Doyle, Sigmund Freud, Carl Jung, and Sir William Crookes were members at one time.

The Society of Psychical Research formed six different committees — hypnotism and clairvoyance; telepathy; sensitives; mediums; ghosts and hauntings; and records and archives — and created scientific methodologies for their field investigations that were considered painstakingly tedious and meticulous in their processes. This kept many prominent Spiritualists from joining the society. However, those who were seriously interested in the phenomenon found it to be the perfect place to study the growing theories on how spirit communication worked.

Through their field investigations, The Society of Psychical Research discredited many mediums and had them brought to justice. However, there were those mediums that were deemed credible and later were called out as charlatans. The Fox Sisters, who were investigated by the society but found to be authentic, later confessed that they were frauds. Other mediums followed the same plight. One of the founding members, Fredrick Meyers, was involved in sex scandal with a psychic investigator that tarnished the reputation of the group. By the 1900s the group suffered scrutiny and decided to perform less field investigations and stuck to experiments in a laboratory setting. An American chapter of The Society called the American Society for Psychical Research was founded in 1885. Both groups are still active today.

Part II

Haunted Cities

This book is written for people who are curious about some of the most haunted spots in Arizona. Whether you are a newbie or a seasoned professional paranormal investigator there is something in this book for you. If you are not a paranormal investigator and you just want to hang out in restaurant with ghosts or sleep in a haunted hotel, then you will have more than enough locations to choose from.

Locations are grouped by city in no particular order. I visited as many locations as I possibly could. There were places that I definitely felt were haunted and others that were as quiet and soothing as a library. I have been as honest and thorough about my experiences as possible to give the most accurate portrayal of the paranormal activity in the location. In some cases, I have added the experiences of other investigators in their own words if I thought it was pertinent to the location.

I intentionally did not rate the paranormal activity I experienced at a location. Just because I had a paranormal experience in a location does not guarantee that you will have one. On the flip side of that, just because I didn't have an experience doesn't mean that you won't. There are numerous amounts of variables that go into a haunting so it's hard to predict when a paranormal event will manifest.

At all the places, I used the technical investigative process and the psychic approach to show that you can glean positive results from both types of paranormal investigations. Some investigations were with my paranormal team, Paranormal Investigators of Southern Arizona (P.I.S.A.) using a strict protocol; other times I went by myself, using my sixth sense as my only tool.

When visiting a haunted location, make sure you ask about the ghost stories circulating. Some of the more haunted hotels have ghost journals at the front counter where guests have written down their experiences while staying at the hotel. Most staff is more than happy to tell you their ghostly tales. It is best to go in with optimism and a healthy sense of adventure.

I have learned more from inquiring the staff about a location than I ever have by researching online and going it alone. If you ask, a lot of times the staff or management will gladly take you around and show you the prime spots for paranormal activity or they will let you wander about the establishment even if you choose not to stay. You can never go wrong with a good attitude.

Always be mindful of a location even if the management is totally gung-ho about paranormal investigations and is giving you free reign of the place. First and foremost an establishment with paranormal activity is there to make money on their paying clientele who are not there to investigate ghosts. There are those few hotels that advertise specifically to clientele interested in paranormal activity, but it isn't the norm.

Being straightforward about your intentions and asking permission to investigate is essential. Make sure you know what the guidelines are and most importantly follow them. I have been to a number of locations where they were open to paranormal investigators until a team came in and didn't follow the rules. Remember, you are an example for the rest of the paranormal world. Sad but true, all it takes is one bad experience to ruin it for everyone.

When investigating, feel free to use your own methodology, but make sure you know why you are using a certain technique and the theories behind them. For example, don't just carry around an electromagnetic field detector and use it in your investigation. Take the time to understand how the gadget works and why it used to detect paranormal activity. If you are merely going to be using your sixth sense, make sure you have an understanding of basic psi phenomenon and psychic protection. For your convenience, there are sections on the basic tools for paranormal investigating, psi phenomenon terminology, near death terminology, and basic psychic protection procedures in the back of this book.

Above all else be safe and have fun.

Happy Haunting!

Tucson

Like much of the West, the first settlers in Tucson were the Paleo Indians. Dating back to 1000 B.C., archeological excavations have located agricultural settlements along the Santa Cruz River. Later, the Hohokam tribes settled in the region. They were farmers growing corn and beans and hunted the native wild life. The tribe was especially known for their red-on-brown pottery methods.

Around 1540, Francisco Coronado led his Spaniard expedition through Tucson searching for the Seven Cities of Gold. In 1692, Eusebio Francisco Kino, a Catholic priest, traveled the Southwest setting up missions to convert the Indians to Christianity and, in 1700, founded the Mission Xavier del Bac in an area seven miles upstream from the small Tucson settlement.

Eventually, Tucson became an official territory claimed by the Spaniards on August 20, 1775 by Colonel Hugo O'Coner. Under his reign, the Spanish Army built a fort to house soldier settlers and other travelers. The fort was called El Presidio San Augustin del Tucson and was created as part of Spain's stake to claim of the northern territories for the New Spain. In its prime the presidio covered more than eleven acres and included a chapel, a cemetery, two plazas, stables, and housing quarters. At first a wood palisade enclosed the fort, but an Apache assault proved that something stronger was needed, so the soldiers erected an eight to twelve-foot adobe wall to keep out unwanted attacks.

When Mexico gained independence from Spain in 1821, the new country took claim of the presidio and shortened the name of the settlement to Tucson. Mexico had control of the area until 1853; at that time, it was given to the United States as part of the Gasden Purchase. However, American soldiers did not officially stake claim and set up camp in Tucson until 1856.

By the 1900s, Tucson was a thriving city with a population of approximately 7,500 people. Around this time the US Veterans Administration commissioned the construction of a Veterans Hospital to accommodate World War I veterans with respiratory problems from chemical warfare. It was thought that the clean, dry air would help with their respiratory therapy.

Through the years, the population has grown exponentially. Now, the city of Tucson holds nearly 1 million people.

The Boot Man on "A" Mountain

I have no idea how I ended up living in Tucson. Some days I wake up and have to consciously recall that I live in the desert. I mean, I remember trudging my belongings across the state divider from California to Arizona in a rental. My soon-to-be ex-husband was nice enough to keep me company on the long ten-hour trip.

Unfortunately, we hit traffic in Los Angeles. The accordion flow cars hurled my stomach in nausea-mode from which I never returned. I spent a good portion of the trip focusing on keeping the contents of my stomach IN my stomach and the other portion spewing all over the highway. I had a rather unfortunate mishap with partially digested taco salad in Phoenix that keeps me from ever eating them again. It's a good thing that my ex-husband and I have known each other since the better part of the 90s or else this might have put him off me forever, and just because I know you're thinking it, no, he did not divorce me because of that trip; although, I would have totally understood.

We reached my mother's house around 2 a.m. and I greeted her with more throwing-up. I made it to the mattress she had put on her living room floor for us. As soon as I hit the makeshift bed, my eyes closed and I passed out. The next morning I awoke wondering where the heck I was and the tradition has stuck over two years later.

Tucson is much different than my hometown. The most obvious terrain difference is the ocean. There isn't one. Most days the sky is brilliant blue with the sun's blazing rays oppressively beating down on everything in its path. There's dust persistently in the air and cloud-cover is a luxury. The air is brittle from lack of moisture — until the rains come sporadically. When it rains it heaves buckets of water from the heavens for about ten minutes and then it stops just as abruptly. Thunder claps and lightning streaks the horizon with a majestic power fitting of the Gods and Goddesses, but mostly, it's sun and heat and dryness. Did I mention the sun?

It's such a different climate than where I grew up in sunny California where people complain when the weather drops under 60 or creeps above 72. August was the only time it got hot and that's when the humidity got up in the 80s. Yes, I was spoiled rotten, so it was a humongous change to live in a location where it's considered a nice warm day if it stays under 100 and it's cold at 72.

It's not just the weather either. There are creepy, crawly, slithery things all over the place. There are poisonous snakes and wild pigs and tarantulas and lizards and buzzing bugs everywhere. Even in the city. No matter where you go there are animals lurking, wanting to co-habitate with you and share your space. I'm not with good people, but I am especially horrible with anything small, fast and in the cold-blooded family. I can't tell you the amount of times I've seen a lizard in my house and screamed like a banshee. One time in the dark of night I opened my door and I heard something graze past my ear, hit my shoulder and plop on my carpet. I looked down to sight of a large albino lizard darting into my living room toward my bedroom. Frantic, I searched for it hoping it wouldn't climb into my bed.

After I had searched underneath and behind all of my furniture, I figured the evil white lizard had hid somewhere dark and would stay there forever until it desiccated into dust and I could just vacuum it up. With my delusions of grandeur, I relaxed on my bed to watch some indulgent "reality" TV. Some time went by and I had completely forgotten about my little albino roommate, until he ran over my legs and across my bed. It was one of the single most terrifying moments in my entire life. I did not feel safe in my house anymore. My plan was to sleep on the couch with the light on, but then I realized that my couch was off-white and the evil creature of death could blend in with it and cozy up to me in the middle of the night. I shuddered at that frightening thought and considered driving to my mom's house for the night or even going to a hotel, but I was already in my pajamas and the idea of going outside into the cold deterred me from leaving. In the end, laziness prevailed and I slept on top of my covers with the bathroom light on. A few days went by and I didn't have any other visitations from the albino demon spawn. Eventually, he made his way back into the living room and I shuffled him back outside onto the front porch and slammed the door behind me.

Needless to say, I am not a fan of nature. I am a city girl — lover of asphalt and stoplights and sprinklers and convenient stores. They have all those things in Tucson but with the added bonus of dirt and cactus and creepy creatures. It took some getting to use to and I'm still not quite sure if I am okay with the terrain or the ruggedness. Now, I just deal with it. Okay, really, I just live closer to a convenient store.

I grew up in Ventura County, which is infested with ghosts and is probably one of the most haunted locations in the United States, so I am used to haunted buildings and mischievous ghosts. I have had flashlights levitate off the ground and hurl themselves at me. I have been slopped with a viscous substance that I can only describe as ectoplasm. I have been tapped, touched and blown on. I have seen real orbs of light flash across the atmosphere. I have heard disembodied voices cry for help and the sound of footsteps walk across the very floor I was standing. I thought I was immune to it all — until I came to Tucson.

One of the very first paranormal experiences I had in Tucson was against my will. No, I didn't get dragged kicking and screaming, but it almost felt like it. If you haven't figured it out yet, I really like my pajamas. It's the single biggest perk of being a writer. Many days I don't even bother to get dressed. In fact, right now, I am writing this snuggled on my couch in my pajamas. Don't get me wrong. I work hard. Just in sweats and a baggy t-shirt with my hair stuck in a banana clip. Glamorous!

I was spending the night at my mom's house for whatever reason. Being new and single, sometimes I liked going over to my mom's just to feel a less home sick. It was after midnight and I had just gotten into my nightclothes and wrapped the blankets around me. I was comfortable and in a warm cocoon of happiness — until my sister, Rachel, turned on the light and asked me if I was awake.

Now, one would think if you walk into a room and the light is off and you see a silhouette of someone curled up in bed, it would be obvious that the person was either asleep or near sleep. However, there's this weird, illogical lack of boundaries that happens between siblings no matter their age, and common sense goes out the window. Blinded by the piercing overhead light, I told me sister that I was not awake and silently hoped that an albino lizard would jump on her head and nest in her dreads.

Oblivious, Rachel asked if I would talk to her friend who wanted to ask me questions about his haunted house. I side-eyed here with hatred, but the words "haunted" and "house" had gotten my attention, so I redressed and trudged out into the living room wearing my unflattering but comfortable crocs.

Honestly, I don't remember the guy's name. It was the one and only time I met him. He was dressed too nice to be sitting in my mother's living room that's for sure. He reeked of businessman from his short-cropped black hair to his black button-down shirt and suit slacks. A dark leather belt and dress shoes completed the outfit.

Half-awake, I said my hellos. We did the meet and greet portion of the evening and I got right into meat of the matter. I asked him what was going on with his house. With the exuberance of a Chihuahua, the guy went into manic mode and blurted out a series of odd events surrounding the house. He gestured wildly and moved around a lot. It was like he had stored all of the stories in the back of his head somewhere and the release of having someone take it seriously fueled his mouth to move at the speed of light. I listened to him talk and pace around the room like a wind-up toy, letting him get all of the stored information out of his system.

From his diatribe, I was able to gather pertinent information about the paranormal activity. The house was located in a community of older houses built at the base of the Sentinel Peak near "A" mountain. He had just bought it and was in the middle of renovations. Sometimes the guy stayed at the house, but he had other properties and a business to run. One of his relatives stayed in the building full time.

Most of the paranormal phenomenon was typical of a haunting, including disembodied footsteps, the feeling of being watched, things being moved around, and weird noises. This sort of stuff is standard and I thought it was going to be another open-and-shut case where the activity increased until the renovations were over and then it diminished into something bearable.

However, the story took an interesting turn. The owner of the house said that from surface streets he could look up at his house tucked at the base of the mountains and see a plain view of the balcony that went into his living room. In the middle of the afternoon, he was driving to the property with his girlfriend in the passenger side. From the street, when he searched for his balcony he saw a tall man in period clothing wearing large boots standing at the railing. Just to be clear he was seeing the man, he asked his girlfriend for verification. She confirmed that there was a man on their balcony.

Immediately, he called the police and sped up to the house. Within five minutes a squad car parked in front of the residence. Two policemen inquired about the situation and they asked the owner and his girlfriend to wait while they searched the house. They walked around to the back of the property hoping to catch the man off-guard, but no one was there. The police went to the front door and it was locked. They asked the owner if he would unlock the door. Searching the house, the police didn't find a person or even any evidence of a break-in.

The owner was asked to go into the house and search around for anything that looked out-of-place, but everything was exactly how he left it. Perplexed, he thanked the police and they left. He also added that the officers thought he was nuts. From that point on he said there was a large, dark menacing figure that walked through house.

The structure had two levels since it was built into the mountain. The first level had the living room, kitchen, and bedrooms. Descending stairs led to the other part of the house, which was mostly comprised of a small living space and two bedrooms. The owner's relative lived in the bottom half of the house. He told my sister's friend that at night someone with (what sounded like) heavy boots kept pacing through the top half of the residence. There were other guests of the house who started to hear the footsteps too. They felt that it was male who was angry or had a strong energy. This was after the incident with the police, but my sister's friend didn't tell anyone about it. Everyone seemed to be witnessing the same phenomenon separately.

After awhile the owner's relative didn't feel safe living in the residence anymore. However, he stayed as a favor until the house was finished being renovated. The owner stated that he loved the view of the city the house had to offer, but as soon as it was finished he was probably going to flip it. He wasn't prepared to live in a haunted house.

After my sister's friend had wound down, he asked if we would be willing to drive up to the house to take a look. By this time it was well into the early morning and I was running on empty. I told him I could look at it another time during waking hours. He promised me the property was really close and it wouldn't take any longer than an hour.

Slightly curious, I put aside my sleepiness and went along for the ride. The drive was only about five minutes from my mom's home. When he hit the surface street where he looked up to see phantom man, he asked us to witness how easy it was to see his balcony even in the dark of night. He was right. It was clearly visible and in plain sight from the angle of the street. There was no way you could mistake what you saw — especially a tall man in period clothing.

The car climbed up the side of the mountain and we parked in the sidecar garage. The view of the city lights was spectacular and I could see how easily one could fall in love with the property…that is if it didn't feel like death. Even before going into the actual house, I felt a sinister energy and questioned whether or not it necessary to go inside. The inside of the house didn't feel any better.

The house was sparse of material comforts. Plastic hung from the walls and closed paint cans littered the floor. There were tools and materials strewn about in every direction. The house had many windows that looked out to the view, which was supposed to give it an airy quality. Instead, the residence had a heavy, claustrophobic feeling that had my senses in hyper-vigilance mode.

The owner gave my sister and I a tour of the property. We kept the lights off and went through each room one by one. The bottom floor felt less haunted than the top half for some reason, but I could tell that the pacing footsteps were above the residing relative's bedroom and it was intentional. Whomever the looming shadow man was he felt threatened and was marking his territory.

After the tour, the only place left to go was the balcony in question. The owner told us that nobody used it anymore because it felt like there was some sort of weird barrier that inhibited anyone from walking across the threshold. Walking toward the balcony I did feel the energy he had described. It felt like an invisible blockade had been set up between the threshold and the outside. When I walked toward it, the hair on my arms stood up and my stomach roiled.

Still, I wanted to go out on the balcony and try to figure out what the phantom man wanted. Perhaps if I saw the world from his perspective I could understand his motivations. Granting my wish, the owner slid the balcony door open and told me that I could walk out whenever I was ready. My sister stood behind me hovering. She wanted to go on the balcony too, but she wanted me to go first.

What happened next was part horrifying and part comical. I wasn't expecting it and it made it all the more interesting. It's not often that I am surprised by a ghost. I took a step forward to walk over the threshold of the balcony. Instead of moving forward I was pushed backward. It was like two invisible hands were placed across my shoulders and heaved me to the floor. My foot hung precariously in the air. I lost my balance and hit the floor with a thud. Luckily, my sister was behind me and she fell backward with me. We both ended up on the ground, her flat on her butt and me on top of her. Surprised, she uttered, "You just got pushed, didn't you?"

Flabbergasted, I laughed it off and told her that she was correct. The owner stood near the wall stunned. My sister and I got up and dusted off. More determined, I walked straight onto the balcony — I would not be deterred by a pushy ghost. Putting my hands on the balcony I looked out into the blackened sky accented by the twinkling city lights and tried to view the world from the boot man's perspective.

What I saw was the valley from a different time perspective. The dry desert replaced the city lights. A river snaked through the terrain. In the distance a small settlement outlined the view. In my head I heard the words, "This is my land." I felt like I owned the patch of desert below. Looking closer I realized there were rows of crops and workers tending to them. I owned all of it. I owned them. It was mine. They were mine and no one could take it away from me. I had traveled from the South and had laid down claim on this parcel. I had worked among the slaves to plant the crops. I had turned the earth and toiled in the hot sun…

The vision ended as quickly as it had started. I blinked a couple of times and conveyed what I had seen to the owner of the house. I explained that the man in the boots was a landowner and even in death he felt entitled to the parcel he made prosperous. No matter what he tried it would be difficult to get the man to leave. Especially, at how easy it was for him to push me over. This guy wasn't joking around.

Shortly after, we left the house. I said goodbye to my sister's friend, got back into my pajamas, and went to sleep. Since that night I have never seen my sister hang out with that friend again. She assures me that he is alive and didn't get pushed over the edge of the balcony in some weird phantom power struggle. Instead, he moved to Las Vegas temporarily to work on some other properties.

Just recently I asked if she ever found out what happened to the house on "A" mountain. She said that her friend had never spoken of it again and she assumed he sold it quickly after our walk-through. If that's the case, I feel sorry for the new owners. Pushy, self-entitled ghosts are the worst.

Trail Dust Town

6541 E. Tanque Verde Road, # 40

Phone: 520-296-0911
Website: www.pinnaclepeaktucson.com
Hours: Monday-Friday, 5 to 10 p.m.; Saturday-Sunday, 4:30 to 10 p.m.
Directions: From the I-10 East, take Exit 256 toward Grant Road. Merge onto North Business Center Road/North I-10 Frontage Road and turn left on West Grant Road. Turn right on East Tanque Verde Road. Pinnacle Peak will be on your right.

Trail Dust Town is a mock western town located on the east side of Tucson. In the 1950s the conglomeration of buildings were built on the outskirts of the city to accommodate a cancelled Glen Ford film. Even though the movie was never made the sets were already built. They lay dormant for a number of years and the local populace nicknamed the area Trail Dust Town.

Pinnacle Peak Restaurant

Built in the 1960s and being the only restaurant in a fifteen-mile radius, the eatery became instantly popular. With its newfound success, the restaurant helped Trail Dust Town turn from a deserted film set into a thriving tourist attraction.

However, in the 1970s, the restaurant, as well as a good part of Trail Dust Town, was destroyed in a fire. Pinnacle Peak was rebuilt nearly twice its size in a different portion of the property. A security employee named, Slim, who lived on the grounds, died during the tragedy. A large portrait of him adorns the entryway to the Silver Dollar Saloon. Some of his personal articles, including his favorite fringed-leather jacket, are displayed in the large waiting room. Employees say that Slim still looks over the grounds, especially the restaurant.

You Can Check Out, But you Just Can't Leave

My step-dad used to work at Trail Dust Town as entertainment. He dressed up as a cowboy and acted as part of the scenery to give the place authenticity. With a "no ties rule" at the restaurant, his job was to rabble-rouse anyone who had intentionally disregarded it. He would make a spectacle of the patron and cut the tie off of the person with a pair of scissors. There are hundreds of ties hanging from the rafters of the restaurant to commemorate defiant customers and warn others of their inevitable fate if they chose to be rebellious.

The dining room of Pinnacles Peak Restaurant.
Photo by Rachel Woodward.

I had heard stories about Trail Dust Town being haunted and was offered the chance to investigate it if ever I decided to take a trip to Tucson, so I accepted and drove with my sister, Rachel, and my paranormal friend, Guy Jackson, the ten hours from California to Arizona. Since we were in the area, we decided to book an investigation at the Birdcage in Tombstone as well. It was going to be a weekend of adventure. Sleep optional.

Since Pinnacle Peak is always hopping with people — whether it's the staff or customers — the best option to investigate the restaurant was during the day before it opened. It wasn't the most ideal time since the kitchen staff would already be there, but I felt that Guy and I were seasoned enough that we could get around the noise and perform an investigation anyway. Obviously, noise would be an issue, so we opted against using audio recorders.

The investigation also included my mom, my step-dad Guy, and an employee named Nino, who was also a ghost hunter. I had met Nino a few months prior when I visited my mom for Thanksgiving. He was a stunt-man in the live, action show at Trail Dust Town. My step-dad introduced us and I told him that if I ever came back to investigate I would give him a call. Keeping my end of the bargain, I called him and he was excited to be able to conduct an investigation with us.

Guy is an extremely technical investigator and one of the smartest people I know. He has a huge collection of DVDs on the paranormal, supernatural, and UFOs and he has read just about everything on the theory of practice of paranormal investigating. The dude is a walking dictionary. It's cool to have him around most of the time, but it's also a bit daunting since he knows way more than I do and has double the experience.

Nino was a gadget-oriented investigator, as well. He liked to have equipment in his hand at all times. My mother and I have a different style. We like to walk around and feel things out first, then pick up the equipment. Also, I love to videotape all aspects of an investigation, so I'm usually the one walking around annoying everyone explaining they need to articulate for the camera.

With my camera in tow, I checked the place out while Guy and Nino did base readings. The EMF readings were typical with high readings around the electrical outlets, overhead lights, refrigeration, and other equipment. Overall, the feeling of the restaurant was peaceful except for the main entrance. My mother and I agreed the energy there felt strange or a just a bit off, but it wasn't overwhelming.

Coincidentally, Slim's possessions are on display upstairs on the second floor landing in the waiting room. He allegedly haunts the restaurant so it would be logical that the energy felt different there. Nino, my step-dad, and I decided to conduct an investigation at the top of the stairs. Our group gathered just above Slim's leather jacket, which hung from the railing. We had brought a KII meter with us to see if we could communicate with the deceased security guard.

Guy Jackson investigates the dining room of Pinnacles Peak Restaurant. *Photo by Rachel Woodward.*

Since Nino and my step-dad frequented Trail Dust Town routinely, we decided they should ask the questions. Slim might respond to them better since he would recognize them or at least their energy. Within minutes of Nino asking questions, the KII started to blink randomly. It didn't answer any particular questions but it seemed to register when Nino started to talk. After this happened two or three times we decided to make sure that it wasn't electrical fluctuation from kitchen equipment or another exterior source. Nino took the KII and walked around the small second story landing and then went outside a door that went to the roof to check the EMF in the surrounding area. Aside from a high electrical reading from a wall outlet, all base readings were normal. We tried to communicate with Slim once more near his fringed jacket to get the same results and we couldn't replicate it.

I surmised that perhaps it was just the jacket that was haunted. Maybe Slim's spirit was attached to it. My step-dad got permission to take the jacket down from its resting place so we could take it to another part of the building and see if we got similar results. Our group decided to try it in the men's bathroom with the lights off and the door firmly shut. That way there was little outside noise and we could concentrate on communicating with Slim through his jacket. Nino held the jacket in one hand and the KII in the other. The rest of us tucked together in a tight circle. We asked Slim to interact with us through the EMF detector. However, we didn't get any responses. There were no cold spots or gusts of air or anything that seemed paranormal.

From my experience I believe that there may be paranormal activity at Pinnacle Peak's Restaurant. I wouldn't consider it haunted, but I do think that there is some residual energy from Slim's belongings being displayed in the waiting room. Strangely enough, one of John Wayne's cowboy outfits is displayed in a glass case between the entrance to the dining room and the waiting room. I do believe that John Wayne has left an indelible energy print on his possessions and in locations he has resided. I have investigated more than one establishment where the actor had spent quite a bit of time. His energy is big, passionate and a little bit dark. It's consistently made a mark wherever he has been. Personally, I believe that if the restaurant were to take away John Wayne's suit the paranormal activity would fizzle away. Perhaps, it's a catalyst for activity. Like an electrical current that heightens other residual energies.

Savoy Opera House

One of the newest additions to Trail Dust Town, the Savoy is modeled after a western opera house including ornate chandeliers, a raised stage, a dance floor, and upstairs private boxes. Security guards have witnessed dark shadows passing through the structure in the middle of the night and the wait staff have complained that the location is eerie. They say that the place just doesn't have a good feeling.

Trick of Light

Guy, my step-dad, and I investigated the Savoy Opera House after getting interviews from the security staff and some of the other employees about their paranormal experiences. When I asked the staff what building they thought was the most haunted most in Trail Dust Town most of them cited the opera house. Excited, Guy and I were looking forward to getting inside to take a look around.

Guy walked around with his Tri-Field EMF Detector to take base readings. I walked around with my video camera and felt out the place.

The place did not feel even remotely haunted. However, Guy did find a lot of high EMF readings throughout the building, especially behind the bar and near the cash register. There have been studies that correlate high EMF readings with feelings of being watched, nervousness, and even seeing black shadows or apparitions, so the high readings could help explain the claims of the building having an eerie or negative feeling — especially for anyone who was stuck behind the bar for long intervals of time.

The stage of the Savoy Opera House.
Photo by Rachel Woodward.

Also, we noticed that there were a lot of windows in this location. The inside of the opera house was mostly an open, wide space with a shiny wood dance floor and other wood accoutrements. There was a faux white marble bust in one of the corners of the room adjacent to the big glass windows in the front of the establishment. In the dark of night, light could reflect off the shiny surfaces in the room and appear to be moving shadows. With the faux marble bust in the corner, the reflection could take on the shape of a tall person or a full-body apparition.

From our investigation Guy and I decided that the Savoy Opera House was most likely not haunted. The high EMF readings, coupled with the reflective surfaces and the large windows, were probably the culprit for the alleged paranormal activity.

Museum of the Horse Soldier

Phone: 520-296-4551
Website: www.horsesoldiermuseum.com
Hours: 1 to 7 p.m. daily
Admission: Adults $2.00, Children under 12, $1.00

This museum possesses an extensive collection of Horse Calvary memorabilia ranging from Pre-Civil War to the end of the mounted Calvary in 1942. The collections include historical photographs, artillery, uniforms, artifacts, and other military accoutrements. Employees have heard strange unexplained noises, a disembodied voice, and heavy footsteps. Objects in the museum move by themselves, disappear, and return in other places.

Hide and Seek

Strangely enough, employees who work at the Museum of the Horse Soldier have no doubt that the building is haunted. Yet, they don't make a big deal about it. I heard so much more about the Savoy Opera House, which was such a huge disappointment, and very little about the small structure stuffed with Calvary memorabilia. It was sort of an oversight — it was just assumed that the building had paranormal activity and it didn't really need to be talked about.

The museum was the third and final building we investigated at Trail Dust Town. More than a few hours had passed by and everyone had other things to do. Nino and my step-dad actually had to work on the premises and my mother wanted to do other things, so that left Guy and

I to investigate the structure. By the time we entered the building it was late afternoon. Trail Dust Town and the restaurant were soon becoming packed, but not too many entered the museum in the evenings. People came to Trail Dust Town mainly for the food and the stunt show. Most of the patrons visited the museum during the day and took special care to do so.

This was good news for us because, except for one person, we had the building to ourselves. The museum was comprised of three rooms. The first and largest room held the bigger items in the museum like life-size depictions of Calvary men on horses. There was a ramp that goes into a second L-shaped room. It held long glass cases with military uniforms, gas masks, guns, and other equipment. The "L" part of the room was comprised of life-like representations of the living quarters of soldiers in the 1800s.

In the third and final room, an older man dressed as a cowboy sat in a chair in a room full of glass cases holding badges, bullet shells, pins, and other small pieces. We greeted him and he smiled at us. The employee who let us in the building said that the cowboy was hard of hearing and he would probably sit in the same chair during the investigation. He was a regular and we should pay no attention to him.

At the very back of the L-shaped room there were two plaid couches for relaxing. Guy and I decided to set up camp there after we performed a walk-through. The EMF in the building was solid. There were no high spikes and the wiring was good for such an old structure. I took a look around sensing whether or not any of the old memorabilia had residual energy that could contribute to a haunting. With all of the uniforms and equipment around me, I did get the sense of other-worldliness. Time seemed trapped in a bottle and encapsulated under glass. I almost imagined that the mannequins and fake horses would come to life in the middle of the night when no one was there to interrupt the magic. It made me feel a little bit uneasy and creeped out.

After our walk-through, we sat down on the couches and waited for something to happen. According to the reports, things move around and employees hear footsteps and noises. We figured the easiest way to get something to happen was to pretend we weren't there. Some time went by and we started to get used to the sound of the air-conditioner, the street outside, and the small train that goes around Trail Dust Town. We noticed that the cowboy in the other room made little or no sound. Just to make sure he was still alive I walked toward the other room to check up on him. He was still sitting in the same spot with his back turned to us, so I left him alone.

The couches in the Museum of the Horse Soldier.
Photo by Rachel Woodward.

A few minutes went by, and Guy and I started to hear a heavy clicking sound in the same room just outside of our vision. I asked aloud if there was anyone in the room walking around, but nobody answered. We agreed that what we heard was kind of weird. It sort of sounded like footsteps, but not really. The both of us decided to see if it would happen again and we settled in. In the other room, I heard a man's voice. What he said was inaudible and it could have even been a groan. I told Guy that I thought someone was messing with us, so I got up and checked on our cowboy friend. He was still sitting in the same position looking toward the wall. His feet were on the ground and he may have shifted, but he was oblivious to my presence. He probably had no idea that we were even in the building.

Quietly, I walked around the rest of the structure while Guy waited in the other room just to make sure we covered as much of the museum at once. When I came back I reported there was nobody in the building beside the older man. Guy explained that when I left he watched the cowboy to make sure he wasn't messing with us. He said that he had barely moved the whole time I was gone.

Intrigued, we went back to the couch to see if anything else would happen. Almost as soon as I got comfortable, the weird clicking sound started up again. Guy thought the sound was coming from the corner of the room. I got up to check out the display where he thought the sound was coming from. As soon as I stood up, the clicking noise stopped. All I could hear was the whirring of the air-conditioner running madly. I sat back down. Within seconds the clicking started. Guy and I both looked at each other, confused. I stood back up and the noised stopped again. This time I went to go see what was in the corner. Maybe it was the weight of my body affecting the uneven floor or something as simple as that. As I was standing in the corner near where we thought we heard the clicking noise, the sound stopped and then restarted at the other end of the room. I couldn't help but laugh.

The corner where the clicking noises were coming from.
Photo by Rachel Woodward.

Guy figured we were being messed with and we should see what else would happen. Not all ghosts are scary. Some can be very mischievous and like to play pranks. Maybe it's really boring in purgatory or they don't have a good reading selection in the lobby. Who knows. I guess I will figure it out when I get there. Another few minutes went by and we listened to the sound click away. All of sudden we heard a heavy knock on the floor like something had dropped. I walked around the whole museum and not one thing had fallen or moved. The cowboy still sat in the same spot. There was a moment I thought that the cowboy may have been an apparition, but later in the evening we talked to the man and he was corporeal. Just really quiet and hard of hearing. He was a regular at the museum and a friend of one of the employees. Back at the couch, we heard the clicking noise a few more times. Then it just went away. I have no idea what made the sound, but I truly believe the museum is haunted.

The Southern Arizona Transportation Museum

414 North Toole Avenue

Phone: 520-623-2223
Website: www.tucsonhistoricdepot.org
Hours: Tuesday, Wednesday, and Thursday, 11 a.m. to 3 p.m.; Friday-Saturday, 10 a.m. to 4 p.m.; Sunday, 11 a.m. to 3 p.m.
Directions: From the I-10 East, take Exit 258 toward Congress Street/Broadway Boulevard. Turn left on West Congress Street. Veer to the right on West Broadway Boulevard. Veer to the left on North Toole Avenue.

The Southern Arizona Transportation Museum was founded in 1998. Originally the Southern Pacific Railroad Depot, in 1880 the site consisted of a large wooden building built for one of the newest train stops on the Southern Pacific railroad route through the Southwest. On March 20, 1880, the first train pulled into the depot at 11 a.m., an hour ahead of schedule. When the museum took over the plot, they restored the main depot and its three adjacent structures that were built in 1941.

Train transportation would change commerce significantly in Arizona. The route snaked through California taking only two days to reach the remote settlement in Tucson. This meant that goods could be transported quickly reducing the cost and widening the variety of items sold.

The quicker mode of transportation mostly affected the livestock trade. As the Southern Pacific Railroad laid down tracks to the East Coast, meat and livestock could be shipped fast and easily bringing down prices and attracting whole new demographics of buyers. This brought in more entrepreneurs and settlers to the Arizona territory along with the prospectors who searched for gold and other fine metals.

As for reported paranormal activity, a woman attired in 1800s mourning clothing has been spotted wandering through the main museum building. Witnesses describe her as depressed and waiting for someone or something to happen.

Also, the specter of a grumpy old man ambles through the structure and around the premise, and a smell of old perfume wafts through the bathroom and personnel computer area. It is said to be a protective older woman who looks over certain employees.

Photo by Rachel Woodward.

Locomotive #1673

Originally a coal burner locomotive, Southern Pacific #1673 was built in 1900. She was categorized as a Mogul M-4 class and weighed 146,000 pounds. Only 105 of this type of locomotive were made and numbered from 1615-1719. In 1906, the engine was converted from a coal burner to a more efficient oil burner. During its lifespan, the locomotive traveled over a million miles mostly pulling freight to and from Patagonia, Elgin, Fort Huachuca, and Tombstone.

Photo by Rachel Woodward.

Locomotive #1673 was used in the Rogers and Hammerstein musical, "Oklahoma," in 1954. The train portion of the musical was filmed at the now-defunct Elgin Train Depot — a regular stop on the locomotive's route. A year later the locomotive was retired, donated to the city of Tucson, and housed at Himmel Park. Due to weather and irresponsible visitors, it became rusted and damaged. A restoration committee restored the locomotive to near its original aesthetic.

On December 3, 2000, Southern Pacific steam locomotive #1673 was moved from Himmel Park to the Southern Pacific Railroad Depot by a large flatbed truck where it resides today. Witnesses have spotted a massive green cloud hovering over the locomotive or near the structure where it is housed. Also, a specter conductor wearing a dark uniform and hat has been seen sitting on a bench and staring in awe at the locomotive. Believed to be in his later 40s, he is described as having a thin build, short, dark hair, and a mustache.

Wyatt Earp and Frank Stilwell

Tucson was no stranger to the brutal and often callous killings that were common of cowboy life, with some of the most notorious cowboys, including the Earps and the Clantons, traveling by train from Tombstone to Tucson and then onward to California. In fact, an incident happened on the tracks outside of the Southern Arizona Transportation Museum that went down in history as the first killing in the infamous Earp Vendetta Ride.

The Earp Vendetta Ride was a three-week battle between Arizona Territory law enforcement and their personal enemies. Members of the Ride included Wyatt Earp, Warren Earp, Doc Holliday, Sherman McMasters, Turkey Creek Jack Johnson, and Texas Jack Vermillion. The first of many to be killed was Frank Stilwell; Wyatt Earp killed him at the Southern Pacific Railroad Depot on March 20, 1882.

It all started with the assassination of U.S. Deputy Marshall Morgan Earp and the attempted assassination of Wyatt Earp. Morgan was the younger brother of Wyatt and patrolled Tombstone and the surrounding cities with Wyatt and his other brother Virgil.

On Saturday, March 18, 1882, at 10 p.m. Morgan and Wyatt were ambushed by unidentified gunmen while playing pool at the Campbell and Hatch Billiard Parlor on Allen Street in Tombstone. The rifle shots came through a glass-windowed locked door. Covered by the door, the perpetrators got away without being identified.

The shots fired at Wyatt had missed him entirely. However, Morgan was not so lucky. The bullet hit Morgan in the back, shattering his spine, and passed through his left kidney. He died an hour later while laying in an adjacent billiard's lounge and not on the pool table like the myth proclaims.

Angry and embittered, the Earp brothers believed that Clanton supporters had killed Morgan. Wyatt also believed that Ike Clanton was the mastermind of the plot and that he had hired two gunmen to assassinate him and his brother: Frank Stilwell, an accused stage-robber, whom Wyatt suspected of firing the death blow, and William "Curly Bill" Brocious, who had tried to assassinate Wyatt.

Before being accused of stage-robbery, Stilwell started out as a deputy sheriff of Cochise County. Johnny Behan had appointed him in April 1881. By August of the same year Stilwell was fired for "accounting irregularities." A month later, he became the prime suspect in a Bisbee stagecoach robbery that took place on September 8, 1881. The Earp brothers, along with Behan, arrested Stilwell and he was held in a Tucson jail. Shortly after he was arrested, Stilwell was acquitted due to lack of evidence.

A statue of Wyatt Earp and Doc Holliday memorializes the shooting of Frank Stillwell behind the Southern Arizona Transportation Museum. *Photo by Rachel Woodward.*

The Confrontation

Six months later, on the night of March 20, 1882, for reasons that are unclear to this day, Frank Stilwell and Ike Clanton were at the Southern Pacific Railroad Depot. Later, Clanton confessed that he knew the Earp family was going to be in Tucson. Virgil and other Earp family members had stopped for lunch in Tucson and then were put on a train bound to California. Wyatt, Doc Holliday, and three others were there for protection.

According to one report, Stilwell and Clanton were seen with weapons on a flatcar in the train yard waiting to assassinate Virgil Earp as he boarded the train. Wyatt, Doc Holliday, and his posse spotted Stilwell and Clanton first. Shots were fired. (The story changes slightly depending on whether the person telling it is an Earp supporter or a Clanton supporter.)

As gunfire exploded through the night air, Stilwell spotted Wyatt coming toward him. Stilwell dropped his weapon and ran through the train yard. Earp caught up to him and shot him point blank under the ribs. It is said that Stilwell had his hands up in defense. His last words were, "Morg, Morg," short for Morgan as Wyatt had an uncanny resemblance to his brother.

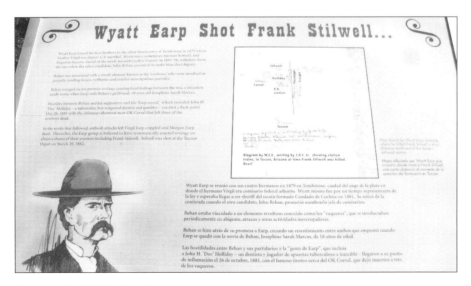

Photo by *Rachel Woodward*.

The next day, Stilwell's body was found riddled with bullets. Wyatt's first shot would have been the deathblow. However, the body had at least three shotgun wounds and two shotgun blasts. The coroner declared that he had never seen a body in such disrepair in his whole life.

All five men in the Earp party were indicted in the killing of Frank Stilwell. As a defense, Earp claimed that Stilwell had resisted arrest and all were arraigned of the murder.

Originally Frank Stilwell's body was buried in the Old Tucson Cemetery, but when the cemetery closed down, he was moved to Evergreen Cemetery. His body still rests there today.

Some say these train tracks are haunted by the ghost of Frank Stilwell. Gunshots have been heard near the tracks. When investigated nothing out-of-the-ordinary is found.

The Fox Theater

17 West Congress Street

Phone: 520-624-1515
Website: www.foxtucsontheatre.org
Directions: From I-10 East, take Exit 258 towards Congress Street/ Broadway Boulevard. Veer right to West Broadway Boulevard. Turn left on South Scott Avenue and then left on East Congress Street.

Ground broke for the Fox Theater on August 2, 1929. Initially it was to be called The Tower Theater, a name chosen by the Diamos Brothers who owned a series of Lyric Amusement Chain Theaters throughout the Southwest. The named was changed to Fox Theater in late September 1929, when the Lyric chain joined forces with the Fox West Coast Theater chain.

The Lyric Amusement Company was a family-owned business run by James N. Xalis and his nephews: Nick, Frank Diamos, David, and George K. Diamos. They were immigrants from Greece who had resided in California making their money by running several successful coffee shops.

Xalis was smitten with the movies and the new nickelodeons that were cropping up throughout the United States, so the family business quickly turned to buying and building theaters. They bought their first theater in Tucson and eventually owned a series of large theaters in the Southwest including the Grand Theater in Douglas, Arizona.

Originally, Fox Theater was budgeted for $200,000, but with furnishings the final cost was closer to $300,000. It was designed for both vaudeville performances and movies with a stage, a fly loft, and full dressing rooms beneath the stage. However, because of the Depression, performances were limited and the dressing rooms were never fully completed.

Photo by *Rachel Woodward*.

There are many ghost stories attached to the Fox Theater. A projectionist saw a ball of tape moving on its own accord on a table. Figuring it was a paranormal activity he invited the ghost to interact with the ball in a more extreme fashion. Upon his request, the ball rolled back and forth across the table.

Also, in the projection room, the equipment is routinely taken apart by phantom hands. Lenses are unscrewed from the projection machine, a piece that can only be manipulated with a special tool.

Outside the Fox Theater, a man dressed in Depression-era clothing is seen panhandling for money to feed his family.

Ghost Tours and Mariachi Bands

I was not able to go inside of the Fox Theater even though I would like to in the future. However, my fascination with the panhandling specter had me standing outside the theater on more than one occasion waiting for his presence. As of tonight, I still haven't seen him. I will keep trying, though. I just like the idea of being asked for some change by a ghost. If I ever see him, I'm going to give him a couple of dollars just to see what he does with it. I wonder if ghosts can shop.

Erik is a member of P.I.S.A., which performed the group ghost tours of downtown Tucson in October 2009, and he had the good fortune to be in the right place at the right time. He got his tour group access to the theater and these are his experiences in his own words:

"At the Fox Theatre, there was a large party going on that had spilled onto the sidewalk. A few of the attendees noticed us and asked what we were doing. I told them and they wanted to know about the history of the place. We were invited in and allowed to go through the theatre at our leisure. Two of the people on the tour group were psychic and picked up sensations around a window on the second floor. One lady said she got the sensation somebody for a fellow ghost across the street. The other lady said the ghost died from going through the window. I picked up that this "ghost" was more of an image and not really aware, that during this person's life he would often gaze out the second story window at a woman across the street.

I was distracted by the chaotic party and an "awareness" in another part of the building. Following my senses I walk up to a door. Upon opening the door I immediately made several realizations. The first is that even older soundproof doors in theatres do an amazing job of blocking out sound. The second is that Mariachi needs to be played under an open sky. I summed up my courage and entered anyway. I pinpointed the source the energy I was picking up. It was coming from the direction of the projectionist room. I wanted to go in and see what "who" was in there, but had no way to access the projectionist room. Instead, I went to find the others in my group."

University of Arizona Campus

1020 East University Boulevard

Website: www.uapresents.org
Directions: From the I-10 East, take Exit 257 towards Speedway Boulevard/St. Marys Road. Merge onto the Frontage Road and then turn left on Speedway Boulevard. Turn right on North Euclid Avenue. Turn left on North University Boulevard.

Centennial Hall

Originally named the Main Auditorium, the Centennial opened its doors on April 22, 1937, to an attendance of over 2,500 people. The very first event lasted two-hours and included a one-act play by Thornton Wilder, a ballet, musical ensemble called, "The Land and Light" and a film of the University of Arizona and Michigan State football game. The night ended with a speech from the university's president, Paul S. Burgess, and a group sing-along-of the anthem, "All Hail Arizona."

The Main Auditorium was a hub for the arts hosting a greater selection of musical talents than other theaters in the area. It became known for the variety of acts that spanned all genres including classical, jazz, and pop music. Due to this the student body of the University started to grow and diversify.

From the 1950s until the early 1980s, the auditorium doubled as a lecture hall. In 1984, the University of Arizona decided to renovate the complete interior of the building. Safety requirements were upgraded including the installation of a new fire alarm and sprinkler system. The lighting, mechanical, and electric systems were replaced as well.

The hallways were pushed forward to double the lobby and make room for a ticket booth. Most of the seats were refurbished except for the small balcony. Those seats were pulled out and the area was replaced with acoustical panels that allowed the sound to reflect off the new material and diffuse into the audience.

Demolishing the original backstage and adding to the building turned the 2,000 square foot stage into one over double its size at 5,000 square feet. The additional room created a large back stage that would be able to accommodate larger productions. The dressing rooms were expanded to house touring Broadway acts and other professional performances.

Finally, the last thing to be renovated in the Main Auditorium was its name. In 1985, to commemorate the University of Arizona's 100th anniversary, the name of was changed to Centennial Hall.

There are two ghosts with opposing agendas that frequent Centennial Hall. Following in the tradition of the age-old battle of good and evil, one spirit creates mischief while the other tries to make up for it.

The "good" ghost has been described as a black man in a suit. People don't remember his profile as much, but they remember his kind nature. The "bad" ghost is more insidious. She has been characterized as woman wearing a white dress and is known for pushing people or tripping them down the stairs. People have noticed the woman specter in the old balcony section and in the green room.

Disembodied music and the sounds of a large crowd have also been heard throughout the building when it's empty. Perhaps, all the good times by the patrons have imprinted their energy in the Centennial Hall forever.

Love Tap

This is one of my most favorite paranormal experiences only because it was so random and unexpected. It just goes to show that the dead are on their own time schedule and they don't care that they are interfering with your evening. When they want to be heard, they'll make themselves known whether you like it or not.

I went to Centennial Hall to see Anoushka Shankar — daughter of Ravi Shankar, half-sister to Nora Jones — a noted, prestigious musician in her own right. Shankar took after her father and is one of the top leading sitar players in the world. Her music has an ethereal, three-dimensional quality to it that deeply resonates with your soul. The night would prove to be memorable in more than one ways.

It was sort of strange how I ended up with the tickets in the first place. A tarot card reader and acquaintance asked me if I would like to join her and some friends for dinner and then to the concert. I was new in the Tucson area and didn't know anybody, so I took up the offer hoping to meet with like-minded people. Well, my acquaintance didn't show up because she was having issues. I was left at a Mexican restaurant with some of her friends and it would have been extremely awkward if I hadn't invited my roommate, Rudy, and a mutual friend, Davey Davidson, to go with us. There were some other mutual acquaintances that ended up going with us, but we had all bought our tickets at different times. So, when it came to seating arrangements we all sat in different sections.

Rudy, Davey, and I had gotten our tickets together at the last minute, so our seating was in the old balcony area. I sat between my two male friends and because we were in the balcony I don't remember anyone sitting behind us. I mean, we literally, were probably the last people who had bought tickets that day, so maybe there were one or two rows behind us, but I'm not sure. From memory all I remember is being near the top.

Anoushka Shankar is tiny. She's a little over five feet and the sitar is huge in comparison to her small frame. She and two accompanying musicians sat in a semi-circle in the middle of the stage. A black piano was stage right. The piano man would come and go as he was needed. Behind the three musicians, there was a complete drum set that was utilized when appropriate. Colors faded in and out behind the musicians on a white background while highlighted spotlights showcased the musicians themselves.

Even from the nosebleed section I could feel the intimacy. The sitar started off quiet and solitary and as each instrument progressed into the piece of music expanded. By the time the drums came into the song the music had swelled into a holographic sound experience that made it hard to stay focused on the earthly plane. I found myself drifting off into a trance state. My aura reached outward and a couple of times I felt my astral body trying to free from my physical body. That had never happened to me before in a waking state and it didn't scare me as much as it amused me.

As I watched the musicians on stage, I realized that something similar was happening to them. They were focused on the synthesis of the music playing as one entity. Perhaps they didn't notice their auras filling out the stage in shadowy rays around them. Being a musician, Rudy was entranced by the lilting quality of the sound all around us. I leaned into him and asked he was seeing the auras of the musicians branching out on stage. He looked at me kind of funny but really started to pay attention to the stage instead of the music. After a few seconds he noticed the energy fields and thought it was incredibly impressive that the sound could affect their bodies like that. I told him that I was having a hard time staying in my body and he said that he was having a similar issue. However, he was more focused on the composition of the songs to have even noticed it was happening. I asked Davey if he was feeling anything strange and he said he had felt a high energy.

Knowing we were all feeling the same vibrations, I enjoyed the concert and just let my energy wander where it needed to go without letting my astral body travel too far. It was liberating to be listening to music with complex rhythms and patterns that essentially did the meditative work for you.

Some time had passed and I was fully entrenched in the concert, mind, body, and soul. Out of nowhere someone tapped me hard on my shoulder. It was so hard that my first initial response was to hit back.

Instead, I turned toward Rudy and shot him a nasty glare. He turned toward me with a look of confusion. I realized he hadn't hit me. Slowly, I turned around to see if anyone was behind me. There was no one in the seats directly behind me but as I twisted my body I did see a woman wearing a large black hat standing to my right near Rudy. There was something off about her, but I wasn't paying enough attention to really catch what felt weird about her stance. I turned forward in my seat and started to really think about the woman that I saw. It took me a couple of seconds to realize why she seemed so weird to me. She was not only wearing a large hat, but she donned a full black outfit from the Victorian era. My heart lurched and I quickly turned toward Rudy to see if I could spot her again just to make sure that what my mind had put together was correct. All I saw was a black silhouette of woman that came and went quickly.

Confused, I sat back in my seat and wondered why the woman had hit me so hard. To this day I never figured out what she wanted, but, like most of the strange supernatural experiences in my life, I stored it away for future reference. After the concert, the motley group refocused and decided to go to a little dive bar where a local reggae band was playing. We spent the rest of the evening playing telepathy games and dancing on the tiny dance floor. The night turned out alright — even if I was kind of manhandled by a Victorian ghost.

Hotel Congress

311 East Congress Street

Phone: 520-622-8848
Website: www.hotelcongress.com
Directions: From the I-10 East, take Exit 258 to Broadway Boulevard/ Congress Street. Turn left on Congress Street (Congress Street merges into Broadway Boulevard). Turn left on 5th Avenue and cross Congress Street to the hotel parking lot.

The Hotel Congress was built in 1919 to accommodate the growing cattle industry and the increase of travelers by train. It was considered charming lodging for weary travelers and fresh faces coming in from the East.

Photo by *Rachel Woodward*.

On January 22, 1934, a basement fire spread up the elevator and onto the hotel's third floor. Using the switchboard, the desk clerk called the third floor residents warning them of the alarming situation. The men fled from the fire by climbing down the aerial ladders to their safety.

However, the unidentified residents seemed to be very worried about their luggage and they offered a fireman a generous tip to retrieve their heavy bags. Later, the fireman read an issue of *True Detective Magazine* and recognized the men from the Hotel Congress fire. They were gang members who worked for the notorious criminal John Dillinger.

Dillinger and his gang of thugs traveled to Tucson to "lay low" after a series of bank robberies. They stayed on the third floor of the Hotel Congress under aliases to keep from being recognized.

The fireman immediately called the police. A stakeout ensued and John Dillinger was captured at a house on North Second Street. The stake-out lasted a total of five hours and not one single shot was fired. The small town Tucson lawmen seemed to do something the FBI and several states' worth of police were not able to do: catch one of the most notorious criminals of all time. When Dillinger was caught, he stated in awe, "I'll be damned."

In the Dillinger gang's suitcases retrieved from the fire, police found guns and $23,816.

While Dillinger may have been one of the more notorious guests, today the hotel boats many permanent guests of the supernatural kind. On the second floor an older man named T. S., wearing a gray suit and hat, is said to peer out the windows at unassuming passersby. Some say he was a gunshot victim of an out-of-hand card game. On the stairwell and in the lobby, a woman wearing a Victorian gown wanders about the hotel. She leaves the smell of roses behind her.

Some say a long-term resident named Vince, who lived at the hotel for thirty-six years, may have decided to make his stay permanent. Butter knives like the ones he used as a screwdriver go missing from Cup Café and staff members have found them on the second floor. Also on the second floor, in Room 242, a woman committed suicide. Residents have stated that the room has a heavy, eerie feeling. It's usually the last room to be rented.

No Show

Hotel Congress has a huge reputation for being one of the most haunted locations in Tucson. I think it's because of the historical significance of the building in terms of the Dillinger capture. Still, the ghostly stories circulating throughout the structure have nothing to do with that particular incident. It just goes to show that history and hauntings go hand-in-hand — one heavily revolves around each other.

I have been allowed to canvas the hotel and walk the hallways of Room 242. I've tried during the slow hours and during chaotic nights when bands have blared. I've searched the outside windows for shadows and out-of-the-ordinary presences. I even went so far as to eat lunch at the Cup Café restaurant hoping to encounter something paranormal. Personally, I don't think Hotel Congress is haunted. I do think it has a significant presence in the history of Tucson, but I have yet to encounter anything paranormal.

The Pioneer Building

100 North Stone Avenue

Directions: From the I-10 East, take Exit 250 towards Orange Grove Road and merge onto the North Casa Grande Highway/North I-10 Frontage Road. Turn left on West Orange Grove Road. Turn right on North River Road and then turn right on North Stone Road.

In 1929, the Pioneer International Hotel was built by Albert Steinfeld on the corner of North Stone Avenue and Pennington in the heart of downtown Tucson. The building stood eleven stories high with the east wing standing six stories and the north side standing only two stories. It was built kitty corner from the family's business appropriately called Steinfeld Department Store, which was one of Tucson's leading shopping centers. Mr. Stenfeild's son, Harold, and his wife resided in the eleventh floor penthouse of the Pioneer International Hotel even after the building was sold in 1963.

The Pioneer International Hotel was the premiere hotel downtown and housed celebrities, dignitaries, and traveling businessmen. During their annual spring trainings, the Cleveland Indians baseball team stayed at the hotel. Local businesses frequented the building for their events, conferences and company parties. Locals stopped for lunch at the hotel during their shopping trips downtown.

On December 19, 1970, the Hughes Aircraft Company hosted their annual Christmas party in the ballroom. There were some 350 guests that attended the festivities while another 300 celebrated in the business room of the building. This did not include the hotel guests who were sleeping overnight.

Photo by *Rachel Woodward*.

At midnight, the fire department received a series of phone calls from nearby building attendants claiming there was a fire in the structure. Some said it was on the third floor while others said it was on the seventh floor. The fire department thought it was odd since the Pioneer was supposed to be fireproof and there had been a number of false alarms in the past few months. However, the alarm was triggered and three fire trucks were sent to check out the building. As the firemen approached downtown the night sky glowed with a bright orange hue. It was then that they realized that the fire was real.

Guests hung their heads out the windows hoping for rescue. Others stood on ledges or on balconies. The firemen did the best they could but the fire spread at an alarming rate and there were too many people waiting to be rescued. Another alarm was triggered and another three fire trucks were dispatched on the scene.

As the fire spread so did panic. The firemen worked diligently inside to help evacuate the hundreds of people trapped in the building. The open stairways were not accessible because they were filled with smoke and fire. The only access to the upper floors was from the fire ladders, which weren't tall enough to reach.

One woman could not wait any longer and dived to her death from the seventh floor. Others realized the severity of the firemen's plight and started to fashion together "ropes" from tied sheets and materials. A lucky few were able to slide down piping that lead down the exterior of the building.

Yet another alarm was triggered, and four more fire trucks were dispatched to the site. In all, over two hundred firefighters helped fight the blaze; twenty-eight people died in the fire. Most were trapped in the upper sixth through eleventh floors. Those included were Harold Stenfield and his wife, Peggy. They died in their beds, suffocating from carbon monoxide poisoning. Many of the other victims were children. Another man died months later from the injuries inflicted from the fire. That would bring the horrific total to twenty-nine. Of those who survived, thirty-four firemen were treated for smoke inhalation and many others were taken to hospital for minor injuries.

Despite the fire and heat damage in the upper floors, the Pioneer International Hotel had no structural damage. Though the building was fireproofed, the quick spread of the fire was blamed on a number of contributing factors. The stairways were wide open and the fire easily jumped from floor to floor. Many of the materials in the interior were extremely flammable including the synthetic carpets, the vinyl wall coverings, and the painted doors and frames. Also the hotel was not equipped with sprinklers or smoke detectors.

The fire at the Pioneer International hotel was deemed to be the work of an arsonist. Sixteen-year-old Louis Cuen Taylor was questioned during the incident by one of the firemen on-duty because he had seemed out of place. Later, he was questioned and he explained that he had gone to the hotel to steal free food and drinks from the Hughes Aircraft Christmas party. During the fire, people reported that the boy helped a number of people out of the building. Still, Taylor had a reputation and people who knew him called him a "firebug." Eventually, he was arrested and tried in court for arson and twenty-eight counts of murder. Throughout the trial the boy claimed he was innocent and just happened to be in the wrong place at the wrong time. Through interrogations he changed his story a number of times even going so far as stating that he saw another teenage do it. In 1972, Taylor was convicted and sentenced to life in prison. To this day Taylor still maintains his innocence.

In 1977, the Pioneer building was renovated into office space. Now, the base of the structure houses a number of retails businesses and restaurants while the upper floors are still used for offices.

The Ghosts

Like many old buildings, as soon as renovations started on the structure so did the claims of paranormal activity. The smell of smoke permeates through the building at night. Many have claimed to hear the sound of people running and a loud commotion in the upper floors when there is no one in the building.

On the lower floors business have experienced the lights flickering on and off. Others have witnessed full-body apparitions. A man dressed in a dapper suit complete with a top-hat and waistcoat is seen wandering around the structure. Some say its Harold Stenfield still keeping an eye on his building.

The paranormal activity seems to be seasonal, manifesting strongly during the winter months from December to January coinciding with the 1970s fire. Routinely security staff stated they have had cans and other debris fly through the air as if it was thrown at them. The upper floors have a heavy, sad feeling that makes it hard to patrol without becoming depressed.

One security guard explained that he had seen a very tall black shadow follow him through the upper floors of the building. It felt like an evil presence and the man was afraid for his life. He also stated that he witnessed the phantom shadows of bodies laying on the floor an elevator on the upper floors. He explained that couldn't walk through them but felt the need to physically step over them to get to the elevator.

De Grazia Gallery in the Sun

6300 North Swan Road

Phone: 800-545-2185
Admission: Free.
Hours: 10 a.m. to 4 p.m. daily (except New Year's Day, Easter, Thanksgiving Day, and Christmas Day)
Directions: From the I-10, take Exit 248 to Ina Road. Travel east approximately 10 miles to Swan Road. Ina Road turns into Skyline Road and Sunrise Drive. Turn left on Swan. The Gallery of the Sun will be on the right.

Ted De Grazia

Ettore "Ted" DeGrazia was born June 14, 1904, in the Morenci copper mining camp in Arizona Territory. When the Phelps Dodge Mine closed in 1920, the De Grazia family moved back to their hometown in the Calabria region of Italy. Five years later, when the mine in Morenci reopened the family returned to Arizona. There, De Grazia returned to grade school to learn English and graduated high school at the age of twenty-three.

Deciding to attend college, De Grazia hitchhiked to Tucson with fifteen bucks in his pocket and a trumpet. He enrolled at the University of Arizona in 1933 and supported himself by planting trees on the campus by day and playing in a band during the evenings. During a concert, he met Alexandra Diamos, the daughter of the owner of the Fox Theater. They were married in 1936 and moved to Bisbee to manage the Lyric Theater, another famous theater owned by the Diamos brothers.

By then, De Grazia had already taken up painting and in 1941, Raymond Carlson, editor of *Highway Arizona* began featuring the artist in the magazine. In 1942, during a trip to Mexico City, after a ballet performance, De Grazia and Alexandra headed to the Palacio Municipal. In a chance encounter, the artist met Diego Rivera who was working on one of his murals. He made such an impression that De Grazia was offered an internship with Rivera and Jose Clemente Orozco. He worked for the two muralists who believed in his artwork and sponsored a solo exhibition at the Palacio de Bellas Artes.

With the momentum of his budding art career, De Grazia returned to Tucson and went back to the University to receive a degree in arts and music. While in college he tried to get his paintings in local galleries but no one had any interest. Instead of letting the rejection get to him, in 1944 De Grazia decided to build his own art gallery. He bought a piece of land on the corner of Prince and Campbell for $25 and built his studio from adobe.

Unfortunately, the artist's marriage did not fare as well as his career. De Grazia and Alexandra divorced sometime in 1946, but the artist was not single for long. In 1947, New York sculptor Marion Sheret walked into De Grazia's studio; his first words to the woman were, "Where have you been?"

The pair had an instant connection and was married in the jungles of Mexico the same year. In 1951, the couple bought a ten-acre plot on the outskirts of Tucson at the base of the Catalina Mountains. De Grazia intended to build a mission in honor of Father Kino who erected the San Xavier Mission just nine miles outside of Tucson. He sketched the designs for the building and set out to build the structure from adobe bricks made from the earth he dug up himself and brought to the sight in his Model "A" truck. The soil was mixed with water, formed and then baked in the sun.

De Grazia called the small mission, "The Mission in the Sun." It had an open ceiling with rock floors. He painted the walls with murals depicting Indian life at the San Xavier Mission. The altar was adorned with a mural of the Virgin Guadalupe.

Next to the mission, De Grazia built a small, modest home for him and his wife and a studio for his artwork. De Grazia's work steadily gained attention and, in 1957, his oil painting "Los Ninos" was chosen to be reproduced as a Unicef greeting card. The holiday card was distributed in 1960 and sold millions of copies. From there, his fame had been sealed and he spent the rest of his life working on his art.

The need for a larger art gallery soon became an issue with De Grazia's growing fame. He set out to build a larger gallery with the same traditional techniques he used for the other three buildings on the property. Again, he got a crew together and started the laborious work of baking bricks. In the front of the building he fashioned a replica of the iron doors in the Yuma prison. The new "Gallery of the Sun" opened in 1965 and since has had a steady stream of visitors from all over the world.

In 1976, as a protest to inheritance taxes, De Grazia rode on horseback with over one hundred of his paintings into the Superstition Mountains and set them on fire. The event was huge news in throughout the United States. To protect his family, De Grazia formed the De Grazia Foundation to preserve the rest of his artwork. The artist died in 1982 and was buried on the Gallery of the Sun's premises. His grave is still marked there today. To date, he left over 15,000 pieces of artwork, including paintings, sculptures, jewelry, and ceramics.

A Ghostly Presence

The Gallery of the Sun is one of my favorite spots in Tucson. I love that it was built by an independent, passionate man who didn't let anyone squash his dreams. Oddly, I am not a fan of De Grazia's painting aesthetic. I find it to be much too religious and whimsical for my taste. However, I do enjoy the overall vibe of the hand-made adobe structures. It's like the artist put his soul into each and every brick.

De Grazia's body is supposedly buried on the grounds. Between the small mission and the larger gallery lies a pauper's grave with his name on it. The small adobe home where De Grazie lived with his second wife is still on the property. You can walk through it. When I first moved to Tucson, my mother and I sat in the structure with a tape recorder hoping to communicate with De Grazia or his wife. We didn't get any EVPs, but I could swear that I felt the residual of his presence lingering in each and every stone of the building.

On another trip to the museum, I sat in a room where a TV played a biography piece on De Grazia from the 1960s. It played in a loop and luckily I entered the room during the beginning of one of its cycles. I sat at the farthest edge in a row of chairs. Less than a foot from me was a locked door that probably went into another room of the museum. There wasn't anyone else in the dimly lit room in the beginning but then a few people sat down sporadically while the film played.

I remember sitting in the chair enthralled by the biography. He had lived such a simple life and it made me think about my own life. To my left a dark male figure about six feet tall passed by me. Instinctively, I moved to the right and even started to say sorry for being in the way. Then it dawned on me that I was in the last chair in the row and there was only about a foot between the door and me. There was no way someone of the man's stature could even pass by in such a small space. I looked around to make sure nobody had walked by and created a life-size shadow. There was nobody in the room and there weren't any people milling about in the large walkway between rooms of the museum.

Honestly, I think that De Grazia's ghost still wanders around the property. I think he watches over it. Other times walking around the museum I have felt a presence behind me or near me and I have looked to find I am the only one in the room. It's a very odd phenomenon, but at the same time it's extremely comforting. If ever you visit the Gallery in the Sun, make sure to look out for the glimpses of De Grazia's ghost. If you see him, give him my regards.

Ed Schieffelin. *Public Domain*.

Tombstone

Tombstone was founded on the will and tenacity of the human spirit that embodies the heart of the Southwest. Edward Schieffelin, a prospector, traveled with the U.S. Calvary from Southern California to set up camp at Fort Huachuca. An adventurous soul, for years Schieffelin often ventured out into the wild terrain of the desert to search for metal ore. His fellow settlers warned him that the area was rampant with Apaches who didn't care about his dream to find lucrative rock. His friends joked that the only rock he would find was his "Tombstone."

Unabashed by the warnings, Schieffelin kept wandering through the rugged hills and mountains. In 1877, his persistence paid off. He found a line of silver ore in the mountains and staked claim on the area. Remembering the jokes about his demise he called the new mining district, Tombstone.

Silver mining proved to be lucrative and soon the area teemed with settlers. In 1879, the boomtown would become an official city adopting the name from the mining district. By 1881, the Tombstone population had reached over 1,000 settlers. Just one year later the mining town housed nearly 15,000 people. Businessman and entrepreneurs came to Tombstone to monopolize on the town's growing success. Prospecting immigrants from Germany and Ireland traveled to the new desert community to work in the mines. A large number of Chinese immigrants also migrated to Tombstone to open service-oriented establishments including laundry houses and restaurants.

Tombstone had a reputation for being one of the wealthiest cities in the entire Southwest. While the silver deposit found by Schieffelin brought much profit, it also brought many law disputes. Lawyers were brought in to defend their clients and negotiate the growing number of lawsuits, with geologists and other specialists joining the ranks to act as specialty witnesses. In many cases, the lawyers and their expert witnesses garnered more wealth than the prospectors.

The fact is Tombstone almost grew too quickly to accommodate the growing needs of the city. For one, the town was quite literally in the middle of the desert. The railroad had not reached that far in the Arizona yet, so the only way in or out of Tombstone was by foot, horse, or carriage. Secondly, water was not easy to come by. These issues became lethal and costly when a fire broke through the town in 1881. Legend goes that the fire was caused by an abandoned lit cigar that hit burned through a barrel of whisky at the Arcade Saloon. Without an ample water supply or a fire department over sixty buildings were burnt to the ground. The tragedy did not seem to dissuade the townsmen and Tombstone was quickly rebuilt. Only to be burned down again a year later.

Water became a commodity and a pipeline was built to pump the liquid in from outside sources. Ironically, around the same time the water pipeline was finished the silver mines hit the water table at 520 feet and flooded the tunnels. For a time, the miners used large pumps to filter out the water, but eventually it became too cumbersome. Without access to the silver ore, prospectors migrated twenty miles away to the Bisbee mines to find work. Slowly the booming city thinned out and by 1890 the population dwindled to around 1,900 people. At the turn of the century there were less than 1,000 people living in the town.

Today, the historical city thrives from the reenactments of its heyday and tourism. Around 15,000 people call Tombstone their home.

The Infamous Gunfight at the OK Corral

Perhaps the most famous gunfight in the history of the Old West, this thirty-second altercation actually happened in an empty alleyway between Fly's Lodging House and the Harwood House. The events leading up to the gunfight are complex. The Earp brothers and Doc Holliday had a long-standing territory war with the Clanton and McLaury families that actually reached farther out than Tombstone. The Earps were deputized and considered the law, but some people felt that they used their power to rob traveling horse-coaches and participate in underhanded dealings. The Clantons were ranchers and the McLaurys cattlemen. The group, known as "The Cowboys" had a reputation for taking advantage of the lawlessness in the remote desert.

There are two tales of what actually happened in October 1881 and the one you believe depends on what side you sympathized with. The Earps claimed that on October 25th Doc Holliday and Ike Clanton had heated words with each other. Wyatt came up on the two arguing and stated that he would be arrest them both if they didn't simmer down. The fight concluded with a threat from Ike that he would be back for Holliday. The next day, Ike came back into Tombstone with a shotgun searching for his rival. Brothers Virgil and Morgan Earp intercepted and arrested him; he was fined $27.50 for carrying firearms in the town. The Clantons version holds to the basics of the story except that when Ike came back into Tombstone he was hit in the back of the head with a gun. When he came to, Virgil and Morgan were standing over him. He was then dragged off to the courthouse to pay the fines.

Billy Clanton, Frank McLaury, and Bill Claiborne rode into town and heard about the scuffle. The group gathered together on Fremont Street near the OK Corral. Virgil asked Morgan, Wyatt, and Holliday for backup while he went find "The Cowboys" and disarm Billy and Frank, who brought guns into the town. They headed toward Freemont Street where they thought they would find the group of men. Sheriff Behan caught wind of the Earp's plans and raced to Fremont Street asking Billy and Frank to give up their guns. They protested telling the Sheriff that he needed to disarm the Earps first.

Behan saw the Earps and Holliday walking toward the men. He asked them not to get involved, but he was brushed aside. When Virgil met up with "The Cowboys," he insisted that Frank and Billy give up their guns. Instead, shots started firing through the air. Clanton supporters claim that Wyatt shot the first bullet, which hit Frank in the abdomen. Earp supporters say that two shots were fired at the same time: the shot that hit Frank and a shot from Billy that missed Earp. Eyewitnesses could not distinguish which bullet was shot first, but that they distinctly heard two go off about the same time.

More shots fired through the air. Billy got hit on his right wrist and he went for his gun. He reached over with his left hand and shot off rounds until he emptied his gun. It was taken away from him by Fly (from Fly's Lodging House) when Bill asked for more bullet cartridges.

Tom and Frank took cover behind a horse. Morgan was being shot at from different directions. He turned reacting to the sound of a bullet and was shot in the back from the opposite direction by either Tom or Frank. It is unclear who actually shot the bullet, but it did come from behind the horse where they were hiding.

Tom half-turned and started to run away from the scene. Holliday spotted the man and emptied his shotgun into his left side. Tom staggered a few more feet and dropped to his death in front of the Harwood House. Holliday threw the shotgun to ground and drew his pistol shooting at Frank and Billy. One of them hit Virgil in the calf and Frank got hit in the stomach but was still able to move. He moved into the middle of street with his horse but the animal ran away from the noise of the gun going off. Doc squared off against Frank and, while Doc was glancing down at the holster on his left hip, Frank hit him. Wounded, Morgan had fallen over a buried waterline, but was still shooting his gun. He saw Frank was

104   Haunted Cities

in direct line and joined Wyatt and Holliday who were firing at him. It is unclear who fired the deathblow, but Frank died of a gunshot at the base of his head below the ear. Billy was the last to go down with a fatal shot to his left breast. The firing ceased.

Sheriff Behan arrested Virgil, Wyatt, Morgan, and Holliday for the murders of Bill, Tom, and Frank. In a thirty-day court case, Judge Spicer decided in favor of the Earps, stating they were justified in their actions.

It's No Secret —Tombstone is Haunted

Tombstone is one of those cities like Jerome — you know it's haunted as soon as you pass through its streets. In the last seven years, my mother, Michele Woodward, has visited Tombstone a lot. My step-dad acted in westerns and performed cowboy reenactments for a number of years. They used to consider Tombstone their second home. Here is a summary of her paranormal experiences in her own words:

"I have visited Tombstone many times and it is no secret that the place is haunted. Everything about the place echoes with spirit activity, residual energy and unrest. It is hard not to feel it. I experienced feelings and sensations that I have not collectively felt in a town anywhere.

One day I was in the Print Shop and smelled the strong scent of raw meat and blood. I asked about the smell and found out that there used to be butcher shop there. Also, dead bodies were stored there from time to time before burial because of the refrigeration. There are spots on Allen Street where you feel coldness. Big Nose Kate's and The Crystal Palace also have their share of visitors from the other side. I have felt the whispers of ghosts and the residual energy in those places like time is locked up. I have also looked at a lot of properties in Tombstone thinking at one point that I wanted to move there. Many of the homes were occupied by a ghost or ghosts and the realtors disclosed this with the information on the house.

I went on an investigation with the P.I.S.A. Paranormal at the Birdcage Theatre. It was after-hours and we had the place to ourselves. There is so much activity in there that you feel it physically. I had to walk outside many times because of nausea. There are energy spots and cold spots. You can hear music playing and footsteps. Most of it is residual, but there are ghosts that hang out there and we heard them.

Also, I went on an investigation with P.I.S.A. at Brunkow's Cabin. I had no idea what I was getting myself into. There is nothing good about that place. It is ridden with negative energy. We had to hike in from the highway and there was a small hill that we had to climb to get to the cabin. All of us stopped on that hill and we were nauseous. We felt this heavy oppression from the earth and in the air. I had to force myself to actually go into the cabin. Once there, I had feeling like we were being surrounded. It felt threatening and I wanted to leave. I cannot say anything positive about that place..."

The Birdcage Theatre

Allen Street

Phone: 520-457-3421
Hours: 8 a.m. – 6 p.m.
Website: www.tombstonebirdcage.com
Directions: From the I-10 East, take Exit 303. Follow Highway 80 for 23 miles. Follow the signs to Allen Street. The Birdcage Theatre is one block from 6th Street on the south side.

Originally called the Elite Theatre, the Birdcage opened its doors on Christmas day in 1881. The establishment was a one-stop shop for pleasure and entertainment hosting a full saloon, a theater, a gambling room and a brothel. It was said that no respectable woman in town would step foot on its side of the street.

The Elite Theater quickly changed its name to the Birdcage Theatre when performers compared the fourteen high-raised cribs to cages. Men paid handsome fees for the private compartments where "ladies of the night" would satisfy their every need. It is said that the Birdcage's cribs inspired the traditional song "She's Only a Bird in a Gilded Cage."

With the slew of bullet holes in the walls and the ongoing parties, the establishment quickly gained the reputation for being one the wildest and rowdiest places in Tombstone. For eight years its doors stayed open 24 hours a day, 7 days a week, 365 days a year. An article from *The New York Times* stated, "The Bird Cage Theatre is the wildest, wickedest night spot between Basin Street and the Barbary Coast."

One of the longest poker games in history was played in the basement of the Birdcage. The game lasted twenty-four hours a day for eight years, five months, and three days. Nobody could get into the game for less than $10,000 and runners tracked down the next person on the long waiting list when a spot opened. Over the eight years, the poker game is said to have made over ten million dollars, ten percent of that going to the house.

The Birdcage Theatre closed its doors in 1889 as a result of the dwindling mining population. It was sealed off with all of its original furniture and fixtures remaining the building. In 1934, the building was bought and reopened. It is one of the only buildings in Tombstone to be preserved in its original state. Today, the Birdcage Theatre is a museum that houses most of the original furniture from its heyday and other relics from the time period. The wood floors, cribs, walls, the stage and piano are all original.

The Ghosts

The Birdcage Theatre is reputed to be one of the most haunted locations in the United States. It has been in at least four paranormal television shows. Most notably Jason and Grant from Ghost Hunters saw a full body apparition of woman in period clothing descend down the stairs into the basement. They weren't the only ones to witness the white lady. In fact, she is one of the establishment's resident ghosts. The White Lady doesn't like to be seen and she spends most of her time between the stairs to the basement and the backstage. On a few occasions she has been photographed. A framed picture of the White Lady is propped up near the large mirror in the foyer when you first walk into the Birdcage Theatre. A man in dark pants, suspenders and a black visor is often seen walking through the building.

Phantom music, yelling, and laughter have been heard coming from the building in the middle of the night. The smell of whisky and cigar smoke permeates the air without a source. Card shuffling, clinking glasses, and woman singing are other sounds that come from the building when empty. Disembodied footsteps of cowboy boots with spurs tapping hard on the wood floors are the most common paranormal activity reported.

The Black Mariah, a hearse carriage with authentic gold trim, is housed at the Birdcage Theatre. From 1881 to 1906, it paraded the dead through Allen Street before they were buried in the Boot Hill Cemetery. A "Do Not Touch" sign hangs from the carriage and people are warned it's for their own safety. It is said that an unfriendly specter haunts the coach and will push or harm anyone who places their hands on it.

It is estimated that over twenty-six people were killed at the Birdcage. Over 120 bullet holes riddle the original walls.

Note: Wednesdays through Fridays the theatre hosts a guided paranormal tour of the building at 8 and 9:30 p.m., with a third tour offered at 11 p.m. only if the other two have filled up. The maximum is twenty people per tour and you must be at least 16 years old to participate. The tour consists of a walk-through of the building with guides citing its history and paranormal activity, and you can bring paranormal equipment. Tickets are $20. For more information, visit their website at http://tombstonebirdcage.com/GhostTours.html.

Big Nose Kate's Saloon

417 East Allen Street

Phone: 520-457-3107
Website: www.bignosekates.info
Hours: Daily, 10 a.m. to 12 p.m.
Directions: From the I-10 East, take Exit 303. Follow Highway 80 for 23 miles. Follow the signs to Allen Street. Big Nose Kate's Saloon is on Allen Street between 5th and 6th Streets.

Big Nose Kate's Saloon is housed where the Grand Hotel once stood. The hotel opened its doors in September 1885 and was considered one of the finest hotels in Arizona. It boasted modern convenience including hot and cold water and toilet stands. The lobby held three glittering chandeliers while the walls were adorned with expensive oil paintings and the floors were covered with plush carpeting. Each room had the finest furnishings including solid oak wood furniture and wallpaper.

Famous cowboys, including the Earp brothers and the Clanton gang, once called the Grand Hotel their home. Ike Clanton and two of the McLaury brothers were registered at the hotel the night before the gunfight at the OK Corral.

Unfortunately, the splendor of the hotel was short-lived. On May 25, 1882, the Grand Hotel burned down in a fire that ravaged the business district of Tombstone including large parts of Allen Street. Only seven arches and the floor joists remained. The rest of the building crumbled into the basement.

Katherine "Big Nose Kate" Cummings at age 40.
Public Domain.

Today, Big Nose Kate's Saloon still uses the long bar from the original hotel. However, the layout of the building has been renovated. The bar area that was once housed in the basement is now on the main floor. The basement is now a gift shop.

The Saloon is named after Katherine Cummings who was a wild, gunslinging, hard-drinking prostitute and the possible common-law wife of Doc Holliday. In 1876, she met Wyatt Earp and Holliday in Fort Griffith,

Texas, where she lived. Holliday and Kate hit it off and started an on-again/ off-again love affair that would endure over many years. Holliday was even quoted as saying that he considered Kate to be his intellectual equal.

Legend states that Kate helped Holliday escape from the law in Fort Griffith by burning down a shed. It is not known if the story is true. When Kate was asked about the incident, she acknowledged that she had heard the story, but never confirmed its authenticity. The prostitute traveled with Holliday and Earp for several months until they reached Prescott. Earp moved to Tombstone while Holliday and Kate stayed in Prescott to gamble. Eventually the pair parted ways. In 1880, Kate went to Globe, Arizona, while Holliday met up with Earp in Tucson. In Globe, Kate bought and operated a mining house on Broad Street.

In July 1881, the prostitute visited Holliday in Tombstone. The pair drank together and got into a heated argument. Wyatt and his friend were suspects in a coach robbery in Benson and Sheriff Behan was looking for any reason to arrest the pair, so when he saw that Kate had fought with Holliday, he offered her more booze if she testified that Holliday had been involved in the robbery. Bitter and angry, she agreed and Holliday was arrested based on her confession. The next day, when Kate sobered up, she recanted her confession and Holliday was eventually released.

The Ghosts

Big Nose Kate's Saloon has the typical residual paranormal activity that lingers on Allen Street: disembodied voices, footsteps, phantom music, the sounds of glasses clinking, and parties going on when nobody is in the building. Witnesses have spotted specter cowboys wandering from the bar and into in the cold night air only to disappear in front of their eyes. Ike Clanton was a regular at the Grand Hotel and some say he never checked out. He is seen walking in and out of the front of door Big Nose Kate's oblivious to confused onlookers.

Silverware at the saloon has a mind of its own and randomly flies off the table. Mannequins routinely fall from the balcony. Many photographers have taken pictures in Big Nose Kate's Saloon only to find that they are plagued hazy with white wisps that have a smoke-like appearance.

The Swamper

Perhaps the most popular ghost of the saloon resides in the basement. He was a handyman who traded his services for room and board at the hotel. Known as "The Swamper," the man had his own quarters in the basement where he could have privacy from the needs of guests. People who knew him said that he was a private man and he enjoyed the dark, quiet isolation his private room. However, what they didn't know was that "The Swamper" had a hidden penchant for silver.

With a pickaxe, the handyman tediously dug an underground tunnel, eventually breaking into on the catacombs of the silver mines. On his days his off and in the thick of the night, "The Swamper" traveled through his own opening into the mine tunnels breaking off chunks of the rich vein of silver ore that lay under Tombstone. No one knows what happened to the silver nuggets that the man hid. Some think that "The Swamper" never left the building. Instead, his ghost protects his cachet so that it will never be found.

Both staff and patrons have witnessed a specter man walking down the halls and the stairs of the establishment. Others have heard moaning and heavy footsteps coming from the walled up silver mine tunnel. Female waitresses have complained of being pushed off the last step of the basement, and another woman felt cold, clammy, phantom hands around her neck. Is it "The Swamper" protecting his loot?

The Chicken or the Egg

I have been to Big Nose Kate's on numerous occasions. Honestly, if not for the ghost stories that I've heard I would never have thought it was haunted by feel alone. I've been in the establishment at different times of the day and night from the early afternoon to the dark night of early a.m.; when it was booming with activity and during quieter times. There's no difference to me.

On the other hand, the second I step over the threshold of the Birdcage Theatre my breath catches and I can feel the haunted energy making my head swim with dizziness. For me, at least, I can usually tell if an establishment is haunted within thirty seconds — it's either there or it's not.

In Tombstone, I've gone on a few of the ghost tours. One in particular was totally ridiculous. The "evidence" was absolutely contrived and the stories were beyond believable. I went along with it because I found humor in the ludicrousness of the situation. However, my sister, Rachel, is a Scorpio and she has little tolerance for shenanigans. She scowled and side-eyed our female hostess the whole time and by the end of the tour our group became persona non-grata. Of course, what did she expect trying to pass off photo-shopped images as paranormal phenomenon to a bunch of investigators who have spent most of their lives living in haunted homes?

The worst part of the tour came at the end when some of the others in our tour group actually believed that the "floating heads" were true evidence of paranormal activity. It just goes to show that belief goes beyond evidence. It has everything to do with faith and intent. Sir

Arthur Conan Doyle is a perfect example of this. He was an insanely smart man and yet his sheer belief in the spirit photography veiled any evidence that showed to the contrary. There is something to be said by passionately driven faith. However, I think a healthy skepticism is actually a good thing.

Later, I went on another ghost tour of Tombstone. This time the host was a man who had lived his whole life in the town and had experience with technical paranormal investigating. His stories were more believable because they were based on history and personal experience. I could draw a line between point A and B. I could follow the bouncing ball and get to C without any grand suspension of disbelief.

As we walked down Allen Street, our tour guide explained that many of the ghost stories circulated in Tombstone have been fabricated by the owners. As an example, he cited the notorious "Swamper" ghost from Big Nose Kate's Saloon. According to him, there was never a handyman who lived in the basement. The tunnel in the lower level of the establishment was more than likely an intentional route from the old hotel to the mines. That way, workers could have access to their sleeping quarters no matter the time day or night.

Now, in my own mind, based on my own non-experiences at the saloon I never thought the building was haunted, so the idea that story was fabricated resonated with me more than the concept that a man single-handedly tunneled into the catacombs of the silver mines without being noticed. Still, it intrigued me that I knew credible people that had paranormal experiences at Big Nose Kate's Saloon. I have had more than one person tell me that they have seen "The Swamper" with their own eyes. They have heard the moans and the footsteps. They have felt the push from phantom hands at the last step into the basement area. I have no doubt they believe they had these experiences.

I don't even doubt that there probably is a thought-form called "The Swamper" that has taken on the characteristics of the fabricated story. Perhaps some ghosts are merely just the power of suggestion that have been fueled by intention and strong belief. I mean, if you can manifest a new car, a new love interest or new opportunity through the law of attraction. How different would it be to belief in a ghost story, intend to have a paranormal experience and thereby manifest it? What if hundreds of people were visiting the same location and intending to have that same experience? Think of how much energy was put into that one intention. What if that energy is all that's needed to create a ghost? Spirits were living, breathing beings at one time. Who's to say that we aren't giving our own energy to breathe a new life into a created thought form? It makes me wonder how many ghosts in popular places are just physical figments of our manifestations.

Jerome, Arizona in during the 1800s. *Public Domain*.

Jerome

Jerome is 5,435 feet above sea level perched on top of Mingus Mountain that overlooks the Verde Valley. The city boasts a view that spans over fifty miles. Originally, Jerome was one of one of the rowdiest mining towns in Arizona. Today, it is an artist community with around 550 residents.

Often called the Billion Dollar Copper Camp, Jerome hosted one of the richest mines in its time. The first mining claims were filed in 1876, when Morris Andrew Ruffener found a copper deposit. After he filed the claim, Ruffener decided the deposit was too remote and non-profitable. In 1882 he sold the claim to investor Eugene Murray Jerome, a New York attorney, who started a mining company called The United Verde Copper Company. Incidentally, Jerome never visited the city for which he was named. Six years later, William A Clark purchased the United Verde Copper Company for $80,000.

Clark was considered a very modern man for his time, and he helped Jerome become a successful mining town because of the amenities that he offered his mining workers. He implemented electric locomotives instead of mules in the mining tunnels and maintained strict safety requirements. Clark gave the highest pay, and supplied his workers with housing, medical care, and medical benefits that surpassed all other companies anywhere in the country. Clark made sure there was transportation into the city by financing the building of the narrow gauge railroad that had 187 curves and twenty-eight bridges in the last fourteen miles of its 27-mile run. Also, he built three swimming pools, a ballpark, and a golf course with a clubhouse for recreation.

In an eighteen-month period, from 1897 to 1899, Jerome suffered three catastrophic fires, which burned down most of the city. In 1899, the city was incorporated to facilitate strict building codes and establish a fire department.

By 1900, Jerome was the fourth largest city in Arizona. It was known as "Ghost City," and had a terrible reputation for prostitution, opium dens, gambling, murder, and mayhem. In 1903, a headline from *The New York Sun* read, "This Jerome is a Bad One. The Arizona Copper Camp now the Wickedest Town." To remedy the prostitution issue, in 1905, The Jerome Town Council barred women from saloons. However, in 1906, after election of new council, the women were allowed to return. In 1909, Jerome got electricity, which was a state-of-the-art luxury for the city.

In 1918, fire once again ravished Jerome, this time in the mines. Highly flammable pyrite burned in the mines from depths as deep as twenty-two miles underground. One fire burned for over twenty years. Due to this, underground mining was phased out for the more convenient pit mining. However, pit mining relied on dynamite blasts that frequently shook the city. Many buildings slid inches down the hill with every blast.

In 1935, Phelps Dodge Mining Company bought the United Verde Copper Company for $22,800,000 and operated the mines until 1953 when it closed down. Phelps Dodge still owns the mining rights. All together, 2.5 billion pounds of copper, 50 million ounces of silver, and 1 million pounds of gold were mined from Jerome. There are still eighty-eight miles of tunnels under the town, some reaching almost a mile down.

Jerome Grand Hotel

200 Hill Street

Phone: 888-817-6788

Website: www.jeromegrandhotel.net

Directions: From Phoenix, take the I-17 Freeway. Merge onto the SR260 and drive northwest to Cottonwood, turning onto Highway 89A. Take Highway 89A into Jerome. Take the Prescott fork in the road and then turn on Hill Street, which is a cobblestone road.

Note: From personal experience, Hill Street is really hard to find. It looks more like a sidewalk than a road. For reference, Hill Street is directly across from the Haunted Hamburger. If you pass it, you've gone too far. Driving up Hill Street takes a bit of nerve and spirit of adventure, but since you are reading a book about ghosts, I'm sure you have it in you to take in all in stride.

Built on top of Cleopatra hill, the Jerome Grand Hotel stands five stories, and was built in the Spanish Style that was popular in its time. It is the highest public building in Verde Valley. The structure was made of concrete poured on a 50-degree slope, and was built to withstand dynamite blasts up to 260,000 pounds of dynamite.

The hotel started out as the United Verde Hospital in January 1927. By 1930 it was known as the most state-of-the-art medical facility in Arizona. The hospital closed down in 1950 due to the closing of the mines. However, it was left intact with equipment, beds, linens and supplies in place, just in case it was needed at a later date. The hospital was never used again, and the building stayed abandoned for forty-four years. In 1970, the Phelps Dodge Mining Corporation deserted the building. The Altherr family, who took two years restoring the old structure, bought it in 1994. The building has been renovated to ninety-five percent of its original state.

The Otis Elevator and the Boiler Room

Installed in October 1926, the Otis Elevator at the Jerome Grand Hotel is still fully functional and services all five floors. Still in its original form, it is the oldest "self-service" elevator in Arizona. The elevator was out of order for a total of four hours and fifteen minutes in the last decade, superseding most modern elevators. It travels at fifty feet per minute and takes forty-five seconds to reach the top level.

In the boiler room, the original 50-horsepower Kewanee boiler provides low-pressure steam to all of the rooms. It was considered state of the art in 1926 and still provides heat with the original General Electric pump motors.

The Ghosts

The Jerome Grand Hotel has been called one of the most haunted locations in Arizona. Throughout its history as a hospital, there have been many traumatic events that make it a rich breeding ground for paranormal phenomenon including a hanging, a shooting, and a patient wheeling himself off the balcony to his death. The building has always been reportedly haunted.

Nurses who worked at the original hospital had heard disembodied voices, coughing, hard breathing, moans, and cries of distress in the wards — even when there were no patients around. Doors opened and closed by themselves. Other accounts reported a woman in a white dress standing out on the balcony.

Today, disembodied coughing can be heard. Fans turn on and off and guests receive phantom phone calls. Toiletries in the bathroom move or go missing. Late at night, a phantom child runs around the hallway looking for his mother.

The hotel maids have reported witnessing a smiling specter of a six-year-old boy on the third floor. Also, they have had lights turn on and off, and doors slam in front of them on their own accord. Some have complained of being pushed or disembodied voices calling out their name.

When the building was vacant, teenagers would routinely explore the building. It is said that the elevator would move up and down by itself without electricity.

The Death Rooms

When the Jerome Grand Hotel was a hospital, there were rooms specifically used to transport patients who were in critical condition. These rooms were called Death Rooms because the patients rarely lived through the night.

Now, as a hotel, the Death Rooms are still used, but have been converted into guest bedrooms, where, hopefully, the inhabitants live to check-out the next morning. Many guests claimed to have heard a rasping sound like someone struggling for breath or a groaning noise from someone horribly sick. Other guests have experienced blood-curdling screams.

The strangest occurrence happens in the Death Rooms when you are asleep. There are many accounts of guests who have had the same dream about woman in a white outfit, presumed to be a nurse, who stands over your bed with clipboard and takes notes. What is she writing down? Is she there to make sure you make it through the night? If you dare, sleep in a Death Room and find out.

The Ghost of Mr. Harvey

Perhaps the most famous ghost of the Jerome Grand Hotel is Mr. Harvey. The victim of a most unfortunate murder, the specifics surrounding his death are still unsolved.

In 1935, the dead body of a hospital employee, Claude Harvey, was found at the bottom of the Otis Elevator shaft. He was the hospital's fireman engineer, known as "Scotty" to the townsmen. One morning, his body was found dead in the basement when the elevator pinned him down crushing his head. After a police investigation, it was ruled out that the elevator killed him. The body had been dumped there. Nobody knows who or why Mr. Harvey was murdered. He was a man with a good reputation and it seemed that he was well-respected in the town.

Since Mr. Harvey's grisly death, there have been many reports of paranormal activity on or near the elevator. Many have seen unexplained lights in the elevator shaft or heard the sound of creaking iron when the elevator is stopped. Some have witnessed the elevator going up and down by itself. Others have been surprised by the shadowy figure of an angry man, or felt the heavy presence of someone on the hotel stairs. Also, there are sightings of a bearded man who has occasionally been noticed wandering around the premises. Is it the vexed spirit of Mr. Harvey stating his presence? Is he hoping someone will help him solve his murder?

Note: A Ghost Hunt takes place Tuesdays and Thursdays 5 to 6:30 p.m., cost is $20 per person. You must be a guest of the hotel to participate, and you will get a 10% discount on your reservation if you book the ghost tour at the same time as your room. For more information, visit their website at www.jeromeghosthunting. com. During the tour you are given an EMF detector, an infrared thermometer, and a digital camera. At the end of the tour, you will be allowed to use the equipment for the rest of the night. All pictures you take will be put on a CD for you to take home.

Sedona

Often called "Red Rock Country," Sedona is an upscale retirement community with a population of around 11,000 residents. The city thrives on its tourism capital hosting between 1-2 million tourists a years. It is located at the lower end of Oak Creek Canyon and surrounded by the Coconino National Forest. Known for its red rock formations, Sedona is said to glow a brilliant red-orange when the sun rises or sets. The gorgeous landscape has been the backdrop for many western movies including Broken Arrow with James Stewart.

Indians were the first to inhabit the area that is now Sedona. They were a tribe of nomadic hunters-and-gatherers finally settling in the Verde Valley. Between 900 and 1350 AD, the Sinagua, a more civilized tribe of Indians, settled in the mountains, building pueblos and cliff houses. The Sinagua were knowledgeable in farming and were able to cultivate gardens of vegetables in the otherwise barren soils of the desert. The women cooked, weaved baskets, and made jewelry from beads made from clay and other natural resources. The tribe of Indians was so innovative they started their own trade route, bartering needed supplies and goods from other Indian tribes in the West.

By the 1800s, the pioneers were trailblazing their way toward the Southwest in search of gold and other mining opportunities. In 1876, John James Thompson was the first pioneer to settle in Oak Creek Canyon. In the next few years, other settlers trickled into the area and by 1890 there were fifteen families calling Oak Creek Canyon home.

One of those families was the Schneblys who proved to be an influential force in what would be the eventual city of Sedona.

Sedona is named after Sedona Schnebly, a hard-working pioneer woman who came to Oak Creek Canyon to settle down with her husband, Carl. Both Sedona and Carl came from wealthy families and were well educated. However, Sedona's father disapproved of Carl and threatened that if the two were to marry, she would be cut out of the will and disinherited from the family. Sedona's love for Carl was strong, just like her character, and she would not be swayed. On her twentieth birthday, Sedona defiantly married Carl, much to the chagrin of her father.

In 1901, newlyweds Sedona and Carl moved from Gorin to Oak Creek Canyon with their two children, Elsworth and Pearl, to get away from family problems. Carl's brother, Elsworth, lived on a ranch and invited them to make a new life in the canyon. The family fit in well with the other settlers and the couple was hopeful that their new surroundings would bring them and their two children some well-deserved happiness.

Carl was an innovative man and he realized there was a need for a post office in the area. As it was, the mail took months to reach the small settlement since there were no larger towns around. If the inhabitants of the area were to have their own post office, then the mail would come directly to them shaving weeks off of their wait time. Carl applied for a postal permit, but he had to submit a name for the settlement in Oak Creek Canyon. At first, he decided on "Schnebly Station." However, the name was rejected because it would not fit on a cancellation stamp. Again, he tried with the name "Oak Creek Crossing." That name was rejected as well. Elsworth suggested Carl name the settlement after his wife, Sedona. Finally, the name was approved and Carl became the first postmaster of Sedona on June 26, 1902.

Life was going well for the Schnebly family. Sedona had her third child, Genevieve, shortly after moving to Oak Creek Canyon. The family settled on eighty acres of land, making their own clothes and growing their own food. Carl made a living selling corn, tomatoes, watermelons, cantaloupes, squash, and cauliflower in Flagstaff. He also owned the general store on his property, which housed the post office. The family built an eleven-room ranch house, which was later used as a hotel for travelers passing through from Jerome and Flagstaff. For the most part, life was hard but satisfying

Unfortunately, tragedy struck the Schnebly family, when their young daughter, Pearl, was trampled to death. She fell off a horse while helping round up the family cows. Sedona blamed herself for the incident, falling into a deep depression, which later caused her severe health problems. Doctors told Carl that if the family did not leave their home in Oak Creek Canyon, Sedona would probably die from the heartache of losing her daughter. With hopes of getting Sedona well, Carl moved his family back to Gorin. Soon after the move Sedona became pregnant with her fourth child, Daniel. The new child gave her purpose and seemed to ease her broken heart.

In 1932, the Schneblys moved back to Sedona. Carl worked in the apple orchards while Sedona stayed home keeping house and canning food. The couple lived a simple, relatively happy life. They were married fifty-three years. On November 13, 1951 Sedona Schnebly died. Carl died March 13, 1954, at the age of 86.

Sedona's Vortexes

The term "vortex" was coined by the trance medium Page Bryant, who, during her stay in Sedona, channeled information that stated there were electromagnetic fields in the red rocks that were spiritual in nature. Bryant was led to certain areas and meditated there to confirm her impressions. Her channeling became clearer and she had positive physical responses to the areas. She cited four main vortexes in Sedona: Bell Rock, Cathedral Rock, Boynton Canyon, and Airport Vortex. The Chapel of the Holy Cross is said to have its own vortex.

A vortex is a funnel-shaped, spiraling energy field seeping from the surface of the earth. A small but strong magnetic field circulates at the strongest point of a vortex. The whirling sensation of the magnetic field has a physical effect on the location, most notably on the Juniper trees that are indigenous to the area and seem to grow near the vortexes. The tree's trunk responds to the vortex energy by growing in a helical spiral or an axial twist — the base of the trees twisting in a clockwise direction.

The vortex energies are thought to be points of concentrated spiritual energy that span multiple dimensions. When submerged in a vortex, the subtle but focused energies aid you on your spiritual journey by awakening the truth and enlightenment hidden within.

However, sometimes during an awakening you are forced to deal with core issues that bring out your shadow self. Old issues and self-doubts may arise. Base emotions like anger, fear, and anxiety surface to force you to deal with those parts of yourself that are hidden and unbalanced.

Even though these experiences may present painful realizations, ultimately, bathing in the energy of a vortex will reap positive benefits — ones that will fill your life with self-awareness and understanding. When confronted honestly and dealt with in a practical way, these core issues are wiped away, with both the light and shadow sides of yourself merging. The after-effect being a more intuitive and attuned connection to the Universe and its gentle guidance towards a fulfilling and prosperous life.

Types of Vortexes

Masculine Vortex

A masculine vortex strengthens the male aspect of self. It is considered the external, projective parts your personality that aide with personal power and making decisions.

Generally, people who have well-developed masculine energy are self-confident, decisive, self- assured, realistic, assertive, possess a strong sense of inner strength and are able to take risks. Conversely, a person with a weak masculine side suffers from self-doubt, indecisiveness, passiveness, and have weak personal boundaries.

Feminine Vortex

A feminine vortex strengthens the female aspect of self. It is considered the internal, receptive parts of your personality that aid with intuition, nurturing, and emotional-balance.

Generally, people with well-developed feminine energy are intuitive, compassionate, loving, sensitive, artistic, flexible, empathetic, and are able to communicate effectively. Conversely, a person with a weak feminine side suffers from inexpressiveness, is selfish, rigid, and is cut off from their emotions.

Balanced Vortex

A balanced vortex strengthens both the male and female aspects of self. The energies of the vortex work to harmoniously fuse both sides of the self to promote balance.

Airport Vortex

Directions: At the Highway 179 and Highway 89A intersection, turn left on Highway 89A and drive west for about 1 mile. Turn left at Airport Road. Drive for about a half-mile and turn left into the parking lot.

The Airport Vortex strengthens the masculine side of self. Its energy balances the physical body and opens the chakras. The Airport vortex enhances psychic energies and altered states of consciousness.

Bell Rock Vortex

Directions: From Phoenix, take the I-17 Freeway north to Highway 179 (exit 298). Turn left onto Highway 179 and follow it passed Village of Oak Creek. Bell Rock should be on the right. Pass Bell Rock and turn right into the parking lot. The trail leading to the vortex is on the right.

Bell Rock is said to be the strongest vortex in Sedona and can be felt in the surrounding canyon. The energy at Bell Rock is balanced and strengthens both the masculine and feminine aspects of self.

The name, Bell Rock, comes from the shape of the mountain that literally looks like a bell. The formation is supposed to "tone" your spiritual energies, harmonizing them into balance. There are intermittent focused spots of energy as you climb the large rock formation. However, you don't need to be on Bell Rock to benefit from its balanced energies.

Many believe Bell Rock's high electromagnetic field acts like a beacon signaling to spiritual beings in other dimensions as well as life on other planets. If you touch the rock while meditating, you may be contacted by spirits, angelic beings, and other spiritual sources that you lead you into a higher level of understanding, harmony, and balance. UFO sightings are prevalent near Bell Rock.

Boynton Canyon Vortex

Directions: At the Highway 179 and Highway 89A intersection, take a left on Highway 89A and drive about 3 miles. Turn right on Dry Creek Road and drive the route for Boynton Canyon. Drive on Dry Creek Road for about 3 miles, turning left at the "T" intersection. Drive about 1.5 miles. Turn right at the "T" intersection. Drive into the parking lot on the right. If you end up at the Enchantment Resort entrance you have driven too far.

The Boynton Canyon Vortex helps to balance the masculine and feminine sides, strengthening intimacy, commitment, honesty, and openness. Its energy harmonizes your spiritual energies as well as your relationships with others.

Considered to be a sacred place by the Yavapai Indians, Boynton Canyon is considered the birthplace of the first woman. Myths explain that she was born in a cave in the canyon and many believe she still resides there and helps maintain the energy of the vortex.

Cathedral Rock Vortex

Directions: *Drive west for about 4 miles on Highway 89A from the Highway 89A and Highway 179 intersections. Turn left on Upper Red Rock Loop Road. Drive for about 2 miles. Turn left on Chavez Ranch Road. Follow the pavement for about 1 mile. Turn left into Crescent Moon Park. There is a $3 entrance fee.*

The Cathedral Rock strengthens the feminine side. Its energy is strong and intense, but calming and soothing at the same time. The Cathedral Rock's energies enhance meditation, regeneration, and strengthen intuition. The top of Cathedral Rock is at about a 1,000 feet and supposedly glows at night.

Chapel of the Holy Cross
780 Chapel Road

Hours: Monday-Saturday, 9 a.m. to 5 p.m.; Sunday, 10 a.m. to 5 p.m.
Directions: Drive on Highway 179 South toward Village of Oak Creek for about three miles. Turn left n Chapel Road. Drive to the end of the road.

Marguerite Brunswig Staude, a resident of Oak Creek, designed the Chapel of the Holy Cross. Staude had a reoccurring vision of putting a cross on the newly-built Empire State Building and it inspired her to become an architecture student of Frank Lloyd Wright. With Wright's assistance, she proposed to build a skyscraper cathedral in Europe. Unfortunately, World War II broke out and her plans fell through. However, in 1955 her dream was realized when she decided to build the cathedral in her own backyard. The Chapel of the Holy Cross was completed in 1956. Now, the Roman Catholic diocese of Phoenix and Saint John Vianney Parish of Sedona, Arizona, own the structure.

Nestled between two red rock formations, The Chapel of the Holy Cross sits 200 feet aboveground. The A-framed glass window is accentuated by a 90-foot cross wedged into the rock seemingly supporting the whole structure. The Chapel of the Holy Cross is said to have its own vortex. Many have meditated in the area experiencing visions of an underground civilization. Also, there have been many UFO sightings near the top of the rock formation where the chapel is situated.

Scaredy Cat

Most everyone in my family is psychic. We all have different abilities and some of us are more open than others. My sister, Sarah, is an excellent medium and automatic writer, but don't mention that because she will totally deny it. That doesn't mean that she doesn't have her own fair share of experiences. She's just not as open about telling them to the world like I am. Recently, I had her on my radio show and she spoke about a hilariously spooky experience she had while visiting the Chapel of the Holy Cross. While I experienced nothing but peaceful vibe she, obviously, did not. It just goes to show that just because one person doesn't have an experience doesn't mean another person won't. Here is her tale in her own words.

"Heather, being my older sister likes to try convincing me it's fun to lurk around abandoned mental hospitals or creepy haunted homes. To hunt for evidence of dead people's souls trying to communicate with us live human beings. Ghost hunting seems like an idea to crash a party I was specifically uninvited to. I always have the internal dialogue, "Do I really want to be doing this tonight?" That is when Heather begins to stroke my ego and confess how I am the best cameraperson she knows and that she really needs my help. So, like any little sister would do I give in and go to the dark underworld of the unknown.

The privileged few who have had the honor of paranormal investigating with me know I am one-of-a-kind. I am the one that becomes traumatized, running from scary paranormal events that just took place. I am the one out of breath and flapping my arms like a chicken trying to fly away. Or during an investigation when the bathroom door slammed (not once but twice) so hard it shook the wall, I the videographer, handed off the camera to the person beside me (Heather) and ran as fast as I could in the opposite direction. Heaven forbid, a boom microphone falls because I will be the sacredly-cat who screams and jumps into her fellow paranormal investigator's lap, clinging for dear life. (That really happened.)

I am not a seeker of knowledge about ghost hunting or paranormal activities. I do not have the "need to know" about what happens after death. Nor, do I have an interest in the subject. My mind set is, I will figure it out after death. On the contrary my sister, Heather, has made her life purpose to dive in head first into the wonderful mystery pool of all that is paranormal and unknown. I do not have fine tuned psychic abilities. So for now, I leave it to Heather; she can go at it, collecting data from the spiritual world. By now we all know I am not the one for the ghost-busting job.

I was on a business trip promoting *The Healing Patch Cookbook* at the Raw Spirit Festival. My mother was with me and my partner Julie. After an eventual weekend, we packed our bags and headed to Sedona, Arizona. Spontaneously, we ended up at Chapel of the Holy Cross. It was an amazing site. The whole structure of the chapel was built into the cliff side of the beautiful red rocks. There was a steep, winding walkway leading towards the entrance. Before entering the church, I paused in awe at the gorgeous bird's eye view of Sedona.

Inside, I gazed at the high ceilings, amazing architecture, and artwork throughout the church. I walked around in wonderment and felt at peace. Most churches I go to seem to have a stuffy feeling. The Chapel of the Holy Cross didn't have any negative impressions to me. I felt quite at ease.

Julie and my mother headed downstairs towards the gift shop. I followed behind. At the top of the staircase a statue intrigued me. This statue was of a person wearing a kilt with what seemed to me as leather armor. In its right hand it held a sword. As I walked toward the statue my mind went completely blank. My peripheral vision went blurry, and I completely blacked out everything around me. It was as if this figure and I were the only two things in existence. I was drawn closer to it, placing my hand on the foot of the statue. I looked up into its dark eyes of it and at the moment the head of the statue tilted and began to kneel down as if it were going to say something.

Reality kicked in and my mind began to realize what was happening. Shocked, I pulled my hand way from the foot of the statue, which jolted me back and caused me to blackout for a split second. Discombobulated, I glanced around the chapel trying to comprehend the situation and, when I did, to no one's surprise...I ran."

Part III

Paranormal Investigating

Basic Tools

Electromagnetic Field (EMF) Detectors

It is essential to understand how electromagnetic fields work in order to properly investigate a location. Most EMF Detectors function in the same way. However, take the time to figure out the pros and cons of your instrument before using it in an investigation. As tedious as it may sound, reading the manual for your EMF Detector will give you all kinds of pertinent information about the device that will give you an edge on a paranormal investigation.

There is a correct way and a wrong way to handle an Electromagnetic Field Detector during an investigation. The best way to get an accurate reading requires little movement. Hold your EMF Detector at about an arm's length from your body. Take a couple of steps, wait for the electromagnetic field detector to stabilize and then take note of the reading. If you are using a single axis EMF detector rotate the device accordingly. Walk another few steps and repeat the process. If you need to take a reading above or below you, slowly move toward the area and wait. Don't take the reading until the meter is static in your hands and the reading stabilizes.

Base Readings

An EMF detector should be used to sweep the environment for electromagnetic fields and to calculate the base readings. These base readings will give you an indication of how strong and wide the electromagnetic fields are in an environment and how they will affect you in an investigation.

Also, note how large of an electromagnetic field your other equipment produces, and take heed before packing your environment with gadgets. Make sure you know how your equipment effects your environment and what their base readings are alone and used together. Without knowing your equipment readings, you run the risk of false positives.

Video cameras and all battery-operated gadgets, especially cell phones, GPS, and walkie-talkies, will render some sort of electromagnetic field. Most forget that infrared registers an electromagnetic field, so the more infrared-based equipment you have the more you are effecting your environment.

Map out your location and write down all of the base readings for any electromagnetic source. Be sure to add the placement of your equipment and jot down their base readings as well. This way you if you do experience any environmental changes you will be able to compare it to your base readings to calculate whether it is true paranormal activity or a false positive.

Types of EMF Detectors

Single Axis and Tri-Axis

Electromagnetic field detectors come in many different models, but generally there are two types used in paranormal investigation: single axis and tri-axis. Single axis meters only measure one dimension of the electromagnetic field while a tri-axis EMF detector are omni-directional, meaning they can read all three directions or planes at the same time. When using a single axis EMF detector, the device has to be rotated on all three axes in order to get a full reading. Single axis EMF detectors are more widely used because they are cheaper and more user-friendly. They have less functionality than a tri-axis meter.

Alternate Current and Direct Current

Electromagnetic field detectors read either AC (alternate current) and DC (direct current) currents or both. Alternate currents are usually emitted by man-made electrical devices such as kitchen appliances, computers, and wiring in houses. Direct current is natural occurring in the Earth's geomagnetic field.

It is important to note which kind of electrical current your EMF detector measures to know what kind of environmental changes can be monitored. It won't do you any good if you have a DC EMF detector and you are surrounded by a maze of electrical wiring in a basement. While you will get some sort of reading it won't be accurate.

Thermometers

There are two types of thermometers: surface and ambient. Surface or contact thermometers should primarily be used for base readings and to find the flow of air currents caused by air conditioning and heating systems. Contrary to popular use, surface thermometers will not work to find cold spots. Surface thermometers will only read the temperature emitted from the point of the contact, not the temperature of the air. If there is an air current in the path of the point of contact, the temperature reading will be an average of the surface and the air system the infrared beam has passed through. This is helpful when trying to map how currents flow in a structure. However, it will not give you any indication of cold spots. It will only tell if there in an unnoticed air current that is cooling down the location, thereby negating a paranormal response.

Contact thermometers are most effective in buildings or other structures. They aren't accurate outside because of wind and other environmental factors. To use the thermometer in a structure, the thermometer should be pointed at the surface. The infrared beam shoots out of the point of the thermometer when the finger tripper is depressed. The red laser you see is not the infrared beam; it's a visual guide for the user to gauge direct the point of contact. The invisible infrared beam hits the surface and the thermometer calculates the temperature of that surface only. Every surface should have its own reading. Base readings are calculated by taking an average of all the surfaces in the room.

Ambient thermometers measure direct air temperature. For this reason they are best for finding cold spots. Most ambient thermometers have a probe for inserting into the alleged cold spot. You can remove the probe and take the temperature of the air to compare readings. Make sure to re-calculate surface temperatures as well, just in case a cold air current isn't the culprit for the alleged cold spot.

Ideally, you should acquire a surface thermometer and an ambient thermometer. You will be able to get your base readings with the surface thermometer, finding drafts and air systems and charting how they flow. Then, with the ambient thermometer, measure the room temperature. With both calculations you will be able to better assess whether a cold spot is true or just an air current flowing through the room.

Video Cameras

Video cameras are still pricey if you are on a budget. However, they are a great investment if you are able to purchase one. When buying a video camera make sure that it has true infrared or "night shot" capabilities. Some of the less expensive video cameras are not truly infrared. The "night" feature opens the shutter letting in more light, which will give your recordings a streaky quality that is hard to watch. True infrared will actually highlight the area you are recording even in pitch black. If you can afford it, an external infrared light source is a valuable asset for your video camera. It will broaden your range of viewing and make your tape clearer.

Cameras

Digital cameras are the cheapest and easiest way to take pictures for paranormal investigating. They have a USB output to dump pictures easily onto your computer and they are relatively inexpensive. The only drawback from digital camera is the shortness of their lenses can cause more orb photographs then a more costly 35mm camera. Still, if you are aware of your surroundings, knowing that a dusty or humid area will probably be a rich ground for picking up orbs, you can easily distinguish what should be considered paranormal and what should not.

Use digital cameras to document the layout of your environment just in case there are areas of concern later. Make sure to snap panoramic views of the location to be thorough. Always snap more than one angle of the same area. That way if there is an anomaly in a picture, you have other views to work with for debunking purposes. If you can, take off the camera strap on your camera so that it won't accidentally get into your shot. Straps show up in pictures as white and streaky anomalies and can be mistaken for an apparition. Also, keep your fingers away from the lens. Fingers are often mistaken for anomalies.

Try and keep your pictures as basic as possible. Don't use any fancy settings or the black and white functions. Complicated settings alter the picture and it's an added layer of processing that isn't needed. If you catch an apparition or anomaly, you want it to be clear and distinguishable and without any question of what it is supposed to represent.

Audio Recorders

Audio recorders are used for spirit communication to try and capture electronic voice phenomenon or EVP. Most ghost-hunters use digital audio recorders because they are lightweight, compact and you can store more than one track on them. The newer digital audio recorders have a USB output, which makes for easy downloading straight to your computer. With headphones, you can listen to the audio track in an audio editing software and cut audio clips as you go along. If you don't have audio editing software on your computer, check the Internet. There are many that you can download for free that are simple and easy to use. Digital audio recorder capture is the most simple and convenient to record electric voice phenomenon.

Protecting Yourself

Psychic Protection Procedures

Meditation

It's a good idea to implement meditation practices in your daily life especially if you are going to be encountering locations with reported paranormal activity. There are many ways to meditate. It's not just about sitting in a funny pose in a semi-dark room trying to focus on the nothingness. There are lots of CDs, DVDs, and free self-guided podcasts on the Internet that can aide you in learning a practice that works for your lifestyle. You can spend anywhere from ten minutes to a couple of hours meditating depending on how much time you have.

Ball of Light

The easiest way to protect yourself before performing a paranormal investigation is by perfecting your ball of light. It's simple. Stand or sit in a comfortable position and close your eyes. In your mind, imagine a bright white light surrounding your body. Feel its warmth of the glow emanating your skin. When you have successfully visualized your white light open your eyes and proceed with your investigation. If ever you feel scared or threatened in a haunted environment think about your white light protection you and feel its rays surrounding you.

After the Investigation

Here are some tips to help further your psychic protection after an investigation:

1. Light a sage smudge stick and waft the smoke around your body just after you leave the premises.

2. Change your clothes as soon as you get home from an investigation. Don't re-wear anything before you wash it or have it cleaned; this includes jackets, hats, and other outwear.

3. Bathe in sea salt to clear off any negative or unwanted energy.

Electronic Voice Phenomena (EVP)

Electronic Voice Phenomena are voices (and sometimes sounds) detected on audio recordings that weren't heard at the time of the recording. Usually the voice directly answers a question or is relevant to the topic of the audio, and the length of the answer is a few short words. Rarely, are EVPs full sentences. If the voice is audible during a spirit communication session, whether or not it is directly answering questions or interacting, it is considered a disembodied voice, not an EVP. The nature of an EVP is that it can only be heard through playback at a later time.

Capturing an EVP

It is important to establish a protocol for EVP sessions that will take account of any extraneous noises and keep them from becoming false positives. The single most common error when recording electric voice phenomenon is not accounting for background noise. When in the midst of an EVP session noises such as cars, other people, pets, and coolant systems are easily identifiable, but if not catalogued, will be harder to distinguish during playback.

When conducting an EVP session, make sure everyone is either sitting or in a comfortable position, so there is minimal movement from the participants. Place a camera on a tripod in a corner (or somewhere in the area), so it will videotape a panoramic view of the electric voice phenomenon session. Later, if you have any questionable background sound, you can refer to the video and try to locate the source.

Turn on the recorder and state the time and date of the EVP session. Have everyone participating in the session say their name into the recorder. This will help match up voice tonal qualities if there are any questionable phrases or sentences during playback.

Place the EMF detector on a flat surface or the floor in plain view of all the participants and the camera. Also, you can add a K-II or another EMF Detector if you wish to ask the spirit to interact with it. Ask questions in thirty to sixty second intervals. Refrain from asking "yes" or "no" questions unless you are trying to get the spirit to communicate through the EMF detector and catch its response on audio as well. Speak loudly and clearly making sure not to whisper. If someone moves, coughs or their stomach growls or if there is any obvious background noise announce it to the room. Or arm one person with a log sheet, a watch and a pen, with the sole purpose of cataloguing every extraneous sound.

EVP sessions should be between fifteen and thirty minutes long. At the end of the session thank the spirit for communicating with you. Make sure that all videotape and/or log sheets are labeled with the appropriate location, and put in a safe place. When listening for electric voice phenomenon, wear headphones. If you suspect a clip of audio is an EVP, send it to at least two other people; preferably one person who did go on the investigation to see if they recognize and familiar sounds on the recording and one person who did not go on the investigation, to verify what you are hearing is an anomaly. If you have them, check your video and/or log sheets to make sure the sound cannot be reconciled.

EVP Classifications

Class C – The voice has a faint or whispery quality, and its meaning cannot be deciphered. The EVP can only be heard with headphones, but does have paranormal qualities such as a voice that sounds mechanical.

Class B – The voice is distinct, and the meaning can be deciphered, although may not be agreed upon. The voice can be heard without headphones, although the meaning may not be distinct enough to be heard without them.

Class A – The voice is clear, distinct and loud, and the meaning is indisputable. The EVP and its meaning can be heard without headphones.

Terminology

Basic Psi Phenomenon

Extra Sensory Perception (ESP)

ESP or extrasensory perception (recently renamed Anomalous Information Reception or AIR for short) encompasses any psi ability that deals with obtaining information about a subject beyond the reach of the normal senses. These include telepathy, clairvoyance (which is broken down into psychic abilities dealing with the other senses), precognition and presentiment.

Telepathy

The alleged transfer of information between two people without use of the other five senses, telepathy is also called mind-to-mind communication. Basically it means that you can "read" someone else's mind. Sometimes this sort of communication transfer can manifest in couples or parents and their children or anyone who are in close proximity of each other for copious amounts of time. However, some have this ability innately and are able to sense others thoughts without any sort of emotional or psychic link to the other person.

Clairvoyance

The ability to gain information about an object, location, or physical event through means other than the five senses, clairvoyance is sometimes called remote viewing or mind-over-distance. A lot of psychic consultants will purport to have this ability. Literally the word means "one who sees clear" or a person who can see images in their third eye. Most describe it as having pictures flit through their mind's eye like snippets of a movie on a black screen; most of the time these images do not come in any sequential order but more randomly.

Under the broad term of clairvoyance there are other abilities including clairaudience and clairguzance that deal with psychic abilities affecting the other senses. In practical application, clairvoyance is usually only used to describe sight-based psychic abilities and the other terms are used for each specific sense even though the parapsychology community lumps the abilities together as a whole.

Clairaudience is the psychic ability to gain information through sound or hearing. By psychics, this ability is often thought to be connected with communication with spirit guides or other higher beings; although, it is not essentially used for that purpose.

Touch-based psychic abilities fall under the category of *clairsentience*. Most who utilize this ability gain information by holding an object in their hand gaining information from it. This ability is sometimes referred to as psychometry. However, some who can perform psychometry gain the information from the object, but are able to "see" the imprints using clairvoyance. The two abilities are usually used hand-in-hand.

Clairguzance, or receiving information through taste, is not as common, but some do claim to have this psychic ability. *Clairalliance* is receiving information through smell.

Precognition

The next set of ESP abilities have to do with time, either past or present. Precognition is the ability to gain information about an event before it happens. Sometimes it is referred to as a premonition. Many people who have precognition receive snippets of precognitive information in dream form. Usually it is enmeshed in dream symbology but there is something about the information that seems more real or clearer than the rest of the dream and is therefore remembered more prominently. Retrocognition is the ability to receive information about the past. It works in the same way as precognition just in the reverse.

Presentiment

Going over the psychic abilities of four of our five senses: clairvoyance (sight), clairaudience (sound), clairsentience (touch), and clairguzance (taste), where does intuition play into all of this? Well, it doesn't. Intuition is more a gut-instinct like a reflex that cues us into our inner voice. It's more like a compass rather than a psychic ability.

True emotion or feeling-based psychic abilities are called presentiment. It is the ability to receive information about future events through emotional response. Unconsciously, the person knew what was coming before it occurred. Sometimes psychics refer to this as being "empathic" or taking on the emotions of another person. Really though, it is just a watered-down version of presentiment.

Psychokinesis (PK)

PK is the direct influence of mind on a physical system that cannot be entirely accounted for by the mediation of any known physical energy. Examples of psychokinesis include distorting or moving an object, or influencing the output of a random number generator. Most poltergeist cases are attributed to strong psychokinesis in a prepubescent girl or teenager.

Survival After Death

Survival after death includes all aspects of after-life consciousness even those terms that are generally thought to describe paranormal activity. The paranormal field has borrowed heavily from parapsychology though most field investigators don't understand the correlation. It is essential to understand survival after death terminology for any type of spirit communication including paranormal investigation. Often, it seems to be forgotten that paranormal activity is a form of spirit communication. Or that it deals with topics of after-life consciousness and how it applies to the larger questions including why we are living in the first place and where we go when we die.

Near Death Experience (NDE)

The first set of survival after death terminology deals with the living or those who have had a brush with death and who have lived to tell their tale. A near death experience or NDE refers to a core experience from a person who has been revived from nearly dying. A near death experience is usually described as a feeling of peace, a visual of bright lights or a tunnel with bright at the end, and sometime it involves looking down at your own body.

Out of Body Experience (OBE)

The experience of objectively staring down at your own body is called an out-of-body experience or OBE. It usually accompanies a feeling of being detached or separated from your physical body. This occurrence has been described in sleep or meditation through astral projection, but parapsychology only deals with incidents that pertain to near death experiences.

Reincarnation

Another aspect of afterlife consciousness is reincarnation. It is the belief that we have successive lives both in the past and the future. A theory suggests that our souls are constant, but as we evolve our higher self develops a new personality that manifests into the physical world as a person. Although in this life we are a different person, parts of our higher consciousness still "remember" the other "personalities" in the other successive lives. These memories are often referred to as past lives.

Appendix

Contributors

Richard Leonard Senate

Richard Senate was born in Los Angeles, California. His father was a painter at MGM studios and worked on such classic films as "The Wizard of Oz." Richard's Family moved to Thousand Oaks in 1952 and he has been a resident of Ventura County for most of his life. He went to Ventura High School, Ventura Community College, and Long Beach State University where he earned a degree in History. He worked his way through school doing odd jobs and struggling, unable to buy the books he needed (he checked out similar books from the library or borrowed copies). He did a year's postgraduate work in Anthropology at UC Santa Barbara with plans to do archaeology.

While at a field school held by Cal Poly San Luis Obispo at Mission San Antonio de Padua, he saw a ghost. The image was that of a monk. This chance encounter changed his whole life. He began to study ghosts and related supernatural topics, becoming one of the pioneers in the study of the paranormal. He has continued his work investigation from that time on. He has appeared on such TV shows at the "Search for Haunted Hollywood" (Fox), "Sightings" (UPN), "Haunted Houses" (A&E), "Haunted Hotels and Haunted History" (History Channel). Most recently he appeared on "Dead Famous" (UK). He is the author of fourteen published works on ghosts and history including *Hollywood Ghosts*, *Ghosts of the Haunted Coast*, and *Ghost Stalker's guide to Haunted California*.

Richard's newest work *The Shocking Psychic Solution to the Lizzie Borden Case* (with Debbie Senate) has also been published, and he leads tours of haunted sites and holds classes on ghost hunting in his hometown of Ventura, California. He also managed two historic museums and served the city of Ventura as a historian for twenty-two years. Richard also lived briefly in Carson City, Nevada, where he investigated several haunted sites in that community and Virginia City. He writes a column in the *Ojai Valley View* newspaper of psychic subjects and contributes to *Ghost Village Newsletter*.

Currently residing in Ventura, California, with his wife of twenty-five years and their nineteen-year-old daughter Megan, Richard continues to research and investigate the unknown seeking answers to the riddles of ghosts and haunted houses. He is currently updating his work *The Ghost Stalker's Guide to Haunted California*. His novel *The Flight of the Hercules* is about to be published in hardback by *Lost Continent Magazine*.

Guy Jackson

Guy graduated with a BSEE from the University of Illinois at Champaign specializing in electronic communications. He also has a certificate in Advanced Software Technologies from University of California at Irvine. His current job is performing system validation for a medical optics company.

His work record spans commercial, defense, and government agencies (including the Dept. of the Army and 2-1/2 years with NASA). Work activities ranged from proposal efforts all the way through to customer support at the component, system and sub-system levels.

His paranormal research has involved personal explorations into the mind/body connection and consciousness with exposure to biofeedback, various forms of shamanism, hypnosis, floatation/isolation/sensory deprivation tanks, and other topics. His casework has involved several official and informal investigations of the *Queen Mary*, alleged poltergeist/apparition phenomena, and others. He's been interviewed on talk radio (such as George Noory's Coast-To-Coast AM); given presentations on EVP at the GhostFest 2006 on-board the *Queen Mary* and was involved with a pilot for a new television show on the paranormal. He is a member of the Rhine Research Center, the Mutual UFO Network (MUFON), and was formerly a member of the AAEVP (American Association of Electronic Voice Phenomena) and the Foundation for Shamanic Studies.

Guy is a Midwesterner by birth, but now makes his home in Huntington Beach, California.

Rachel Woodward

In her early twenties Rachel Woodward studied Somatic Therapies in California. After a near-death car accident in 2001, her life path took a drastic change when she lost the use of her legs. Through her recovery, she rediscovered her childhood love with the arts. Creating became therapy and, as she regained the use of legs, she began "The Red Ant" clothing line. A decade later, she has returned to her roots and is now a full-time student. She is working on combining her degree in Somatic Therapies and psychology with her natural medium and telepathy psychic abilities.

Photo courtesy of Rachel Woodward.

Sarah Woodward

Sarah Woodward's family refers to her as "the miracle," as she is a survivor of ovarian cancer. Her unique approach to healing, combined with raw foods, resulted in a new life of divine health. While most women do not survive ovarian cancer (and those who do feel less than great), Sarah is living proof that balancing the emotional and physical aspects of life can bring unexpected incredible outcomes to assumed impossibilities!

Sarah is cofounder of The Healing Patch Raw Cuisine, a company dedicated to helping people maintain a more healthful lifestyle. Her previous work history in television news has helped her launch *The Healing Patch Cook Book*. In May 2010, The Healing Patch Raw Cuisine will be launching their first DVD about foraging wild foods. Future projects involve motivational coaching and workshops. For more information about Sarah, go to www.RawHealingPatch.com

Rudy Cortese

A full-time musician playing concerts, festivals, corporate/private functions, and a variety of other venues throughout the United States, Rudy has played banjo and guitar for over twenty years. He is the current reigning Arizona State Banjo Champion and two-time winner of the Four Corner State Banjo Championship.

Rudy has taught banjo, guitar, mandolin, and vocals to students in the Tucson/Phoenix area. He is also is a serious songwriter and composer for the banjo and bluegrass music. He is currently playing with "Cadillac Mountain," a popular local Tucson fixture in the music community.

Rudy has opened for many popular bluegrass artists, including James King, the Cherryholmes Family, Allen Mills, Jim and Jesse McReynolds, and Jerry Douglas. He has played with the band Crucial County and at the 2001 Huck Finn Jubilee Festival the band was awarded third runner-up in the countrywide competition. This festival was also awarded the Bluegrass Event of the Year at the 2001 IBMA Awards.

Rudy is currently playing with the bluegrass group Whistle Stop throughout Arizona, California, and Colorado. You can access the website for Whistle Stop at www.myspace.com/whistlestopbluegrass, and Rudy is also currently writing a series of children's books based on bluegrass music. Accompanying these stories will be original compositions and recordings involving each instrument of the bluegrass genre.

Michele Woodward

Michele Woodward, M.A. has a Masters Degree in Human Behavior and Counseling. For ten years Michele worked with the mentally disabled persons in Los Angeles and Ventura County areas. Also, she worked with the general homeless population including homeless Veterans.

Michele has also joined forces with Geshundheit Global Outreach, a sector of Geshundheit Institute founded by Dr. Hunter (Patch) Adams, which encompasses clowning missions, humanitarian aid, building projects and community development around the world.

Independently Michele freelances as an Intuitive Life Coach, substitute teaches with the Tucson Unified School District and teaches part-time Social Sciences at Prescott University. It is her belief that conventional psychological practices combined with psychic energy and median work can aid in the healing process and hopefully be a normal practice in hospitals as well as the psychological therapies.

Photo courtesy of Michele Woodward.

Erik Assman

Erik grew up in a small Victorian town in the Pacific Northwest and is a life-long student of the occult and mystical. He is currently living in Arizona exploring the strange and unusual.

Davey Douglas

Davey is a self-employed artisan. He has a cool dog named Dylan.

Bibliography

Websites

http://en.wikipedia.org/wiki/Daniel_Dunglas_Home

http://www.prairieghosts.com/museum.html

http://www.prairieghosts.com/foxsisters.html

http://www.prairieghosts.com/ddhome.html

http://en.wikipedia.org/wiki/Fox_sisters

http://www.fst.org/fxsistrs.htm

http://en.wikipedia.org/wiki/Arthur_Conan_Doyle

http://www.prairieghosts.com/doyle.html

http://en.wikipedia.org/wiki/Ghost

http://www.prairieghosts.com/spiritualism.html

http://www.museumofhoaxes.com/hoax/photo_database/image/the_
cottingley_fairies/

http://en.wikipedia.org/wiki/Cottingley_fairies

http://en.wikipedia.org/wiki/William_Hope_(paranormal_investigator)

http://www.prairieghosts.com/hope.html

http://website.lineone.net/~enlightenment/william_hope.htm

http://www.prairieghosts.com/cabinets.html

http://en.wikipedia.org/wiki/Davenport_Brothers

http://www.prairieghosts.com/table.html

http://www.museumoftalkingboards.com/history.html

http://www.museumoftalkingboards.com/dials.html

http://en.wikipedia.org/wiki/Tucson,_Arizona

http://cms3.tucsonaz.gov/history/tucson_history

http://en.wikipedia.org/wiki/Eusebio_Francisco_Kino

http://www.traildusttown.com/index.php?option=com_content&view=article&id=46&Itemid=62

http://hubpages.com/hub/Trail-Dust-Town---A-Movie-Set-That-Became-a-Theme-Park

http://www.horsesoldiermuseum.com/index.htm

http://www.uapresents.org/about/about.php?include=about_centennial

http://tucsoncitizen.com/paranormal/2009/10/27/haunted-by-a-tragedy-in-tucson/

http://www3.gendisasters.com/arizona/4828/tucson%2C-az-pioneer-international-hotel-fire%2C-dec-1970

http://www.tucsoncitizen.com/daily/local/21139.php

http://degrazia.org/Splash.aspx

http://en.wikipedia.org/wiki/Ettore_DeGrazia

http://www.arizona-leisure.com/tombstone-arizona.html

http://www.tombstoneweb.com/history.html

http://en.wikipedia.org/wiki/Tombstone,_Arizona

http://en.wikipedia.org/wiki/Bird_Cage_Theatre

http://www.spartacus.schoolnet.co.uk/WWokcorral.htm

http://www.amwest-travel.com/awt_tombstone2.html

http://www.bignosekates.info/history1.html

http://www.goodies.freeservers.com/okcorral.html

http://en.wikipedia.org/wiki/Gunfight_at_the_O.K._Corral

http://www.clantongang.com/oldwest/gunfight.html

http://en.wikipedia.org/wiki/Big_Nose_Kate

Books

Talking to the Dead: Kate and Maggie Fox and the Rise of Spiritualism. Barbara Weisberg Publisher: Harper One (April 13, 2004)

Index